The End of This Present World

OTHER BOOKS BY DR. STRAUSS . . .

The Day God Died

God's Plan for the Future

When Loved Ones Are Taken in Death

The End of This Present World

by

LEHMAN STRAUSS LITT. D.

ZONDERVAN PUBLISHING HOUSE

GRAND RAPIDS MICHIGAN

ACKNOWLEDGMENTS

The publishers wish to acknowledge appreciation to the following for
the use of their copyrighted material.

Wm. B. Eerdmans Publishing Co., Grand Rapids, Michigan, for the quote
found on pages 52-53 taken from *Prophetic Light in Present Darkness*
by Kenneth A. Wuest.

Moody Press, Moody Bible Institute of Chicago, for the quotes found on
pages 42 and 50 taken from *The Return of Jesus Christ* by Rene Pache.

Fleming H. Revell Co., Westwood, N.J., for the quote found on page 61
taken from *The Gospel According to Luke* by G. Campbell Morgan.

Christianity Today, Washington, D.C., for the quote found on pages 57-
58 taken from *Christianity Today* and written by David Benson (April 13,
1959).

Preface

The chapters in this book actually are a continuation of a series of prophetic studies which were begun in an earlier volume entitled, *God's Plan for the Future.* The first book in this series naturally could not cover all the main themes of God's prophetic plan. Nor does this present volume accomplish this major task. Therefore a third volume is planned, the Lord willing.

Chapters 2, 3, 4 and 5 herein appeared earlier in pamphlet form in the *Bible Truth Series.* They have been changed very little, alterations having been made only to update the material where necessary and to adapt the chapters to their inclusion in a single volume.

Appreciation is hereby expressed to Mrs. E. F. Wright of Detroit, Michigan for her labor of love in typing the manuscript for publication.

LEHMAN STRAUSS
1967

CONTENTS

The End of This Present World

Chapter 1

The Coming World Church

A new and perhaps revolutionary struggle has been taking place within Christendom during recent years. Sparked by the efforts of the late Pope John, and strengthened by a large number of Protestant groups, the movement to unite all churches in one universal church has been making remarkable progress. The issue of cooperation among the churches of the world is one of the most crucial facing us today. This trend can hardly go unnoticed as one observes the reports from both Protestant and Roman Catholic sources.

"Ecumenical" is the word used to describe this movement. The terms "ecumenical" and "ecumenism" are derived from the Greek word *oikoumene* which in its root meaning denotes "the inhabited earth." It is translated "all the world" in the King James Version of the New Testament (Matthew 24:14; Luke 2:1; Acts 11:28). It is thus applied to one large religious body whose influence embraces the entire inhabited earth. In the Roman Catholic Church a coun-

11

cil is considered to be ecumenical when it is called by the Pope from the Roman churches throughout the world.

The Dawn of the Superchurch

On January 25, 1959, Pope John XXIII disclosed in a speech to the cardinals, in the Benedictine Monastery at St. Paul's Outside-the-Wall in Rome, his decision to call an "Ecumenical Council." Now let us not misunderstand the Pope's intention. What many people outside the Roman Catholic Church do not realize is that an "Ecumenical Council" is a Roman Catholic gathering to which bishops and voting members of the Roman Church are called from every part of the earth. They meet to deliberate and decide decrees which are thereafter binding upon all members of that church throughout the earth. The point for emphasis here is that Pope John did not have any intention of inviting other churches outside the Roman Church to take any active part in the council. However, he did intend to invite other churches to send observers to the council.

One of the key figures in the early days of this modern movement was Cardinal Augustin Bea, president of the secretariat for promoting Christian unity. Cardinal Bea, an able Jesuit scholar, had been head of the Pontifical Biblical Institute for more than a quarter of a century. The Roman Catholic magazine *America* published some facts about Bea and his relation to the council. "His secretariat was established to keep non-Catholics abreast with council preparations, to receive their suggestions, and to see to the delicate task of inviting non-Catholic observers to Vatican II. The secretariat also formulates proposals for the council on such important topics as . . . the dialogue with the non-Catholic world." Then Cardinal Bea himself said, "The Council's main ecumenical task will be to prepare for an eventual union, God willing, by bettering relations between Catholics and non-Catholic Christians."

But what has gone unrecognized by many is the fact that some Protestant groups were actively engaged in efforts toward union many years before Pope John's appeal for church union. As a matter of fact, the dream of a united church was in the minds of church leaders at the World Conference on Missionary Cooperation at Edinburgh in 1910. Again in 1925, the idea of church union was a topic for discussion at the Universal Christian Council on Life and Work at Stockholm. Then, only two years later, in 1927, at Lusanne, the World Conference on Faith and Order stated that, in order to find a common ground of belief, it was time to rethink those church doctrines and traditions where differences existed.

This growing desire for ecumenical advance led to the inauguration of the World Council of Churches at Amsterdam on August 23, 1948. The formation of the World Council went on record "as one of the great days of modern church history," according to the Swedish church historian, Dean Karlstrom. The function and authority of the World Council was stated in its constitution as follows: "The functions of the World Council shall be: (1) To carry out the work of the two world movements for *Faith and Order* and for Life and Work. (2) To facilitate common action by the churches. (3) To promote co-operation in study. (4) To promote the growth of ecumenical consciousness in the members of all churches. (5) To establish relations with denominational federations of world-wide scope and with other ecumenical movements . . . " Note the terms "common action," "co-operation" and "ecumenical consciousness."

Thus, it is clear that for more than fifty years the idea of an organic union between church groups has been gradually rising to prominence. Peaceful co-existence between religious groups, differing widely in belief and practice, is being constantly advocated. The newest religious fad is *dialogue*. As a matter of fact, the trend toward ecumenism has reached such proportions so as to bring our present generation into veritable ecumania. Dr. J. V. Langmead-Casserly, Episcopal theologian, predicted that by the twenty-first century there will be "a great united church under the leadership of a reinterpreted papacy."

The ecumenical ferment sustained its momentum of interest and influence through the Second Assembly of the World Council of Churches at Evanston in 1954 and again through the Third Assembly at New Delhi in 1961. For Protestantism the World Council of Churches has become the voice of ecumenism. It has increased the stature of the National Council of Churches and placed the ecumenical movement in a position whereby we can neither deny nor underestimate its influence. Denominations are no longer pulling apart; they are coming together! Bishop Francis J. Mc-Connell of the Methodist Church predicted that in seventy-five years historians will look upon the establishment of the World Council of Churches as the most significant event of the twentieth century because it worked the beginning of the end of denominational animosities.

On July 22, 1965, the United Press International released a statement about Cardinal Bea, then 84 years of age, and still the ecclesiastical dynamo of the Roman Church. The news item said that in just five years (1961-65) this man was the one person most responsible for the amazing progress that has been made toward bringing divided bodies of Christendom together. Certainly Cardinal Bea has played an important role in the advance of religious ecumenism, but so have many other religious leaders in both the Protestant and Roman Churches.

The Design of the Superchurch

The most prominent leaders of the Ecumenical Movement have repeatedly and emphatically stated that their one goal is a united church. They deplore the wild tempest in the churches which has resulted in a disintegration into many small sects which quarrel with one another and condemn each other. They maintain that church unity was broken by selfish and sinful men. And so they appeal for an ecumenical church on the ground of our Lord's statement in His high-priestly prayer, "that they may be one, even as we are one" (John 17:22). As a matter of fact, those were the words quoted in Latin by the late Pope John when he set in motion the ecumenical wheels of the Roman Church.

Now every true believer in our Lord Jesus Christ must admit that Protestantism has been split into many segments, and that even among us evangelicals there continues to be a widespread splintering of the saints of God. No doubt there is justification for some of this, especially where doctrinal or moral issues are involved or where there is an unholy alliance between believers and unbelievers. But, on the other hand, one must deplore the unnecessary strife and divisions resulting over personality clashes, the proud ambition for power and selfishness. This sinful separation was lamented and exposed in the Early Church. The Apostle Paul wrote, "For it hath been declared unto me of you, my brethren, by them which are of the house of Chloe, that there are contentions among you. Now this I say, that every one of you saith, I am of Paul; and I of Apollos; and I of Cephas; and I of Christ. Is Christ divided? . . . " (I Corinthians 1:11-13). Numerous other passages in the New Testament aim at those unnecessary and sinful splits among the saints, appealing for unity.

But is the unity which the Ecumenical Movement seeks the unity which Scripture teaches? The answer to this question is an emphatic No! This modern Ecumenical Movement seeks a union which is organizational, visible and hierarchical, and which ultimately will bring all religions under the authority of Rome. But the unity of believers in Jesus Christ, as taught in the New Testament, is a spiritual unity brought to pass, and made experientially real by the incoming and indwelling of the Holy Spirit. The aggregate of all true believers in the Lord Jesus Christ is "*the* church, which is his Body" (Ephesians 1:22, 23). It already exists and is functioning. "There is one body, and one Spirit, even as ye are called in one hope of your calling; One Lord, one faith, one baptism, One God and Father of all, who is above all, and through all, and in you all" (Ephesians 4:4-6). This spiritual entity, consisting of all saved persons, is God's Ecumenical Church, and the only way that one can be added to His Church is to receive by faith Jesus Christ as Saviour and Lord. No one can join His Church, but one is joined to it the moment he savingly believes on the Lord Jesus Christ.

The modern Ecumenical Movement's use of John 17 as a basis of its appeal for a world church is in very truth a gross misuse of that Scripture passage. When our Lord prayed, "that they may be one, even as we are one" (John 17:22), He most surely was not praying for all persons in the inhabited earth, but rather for that select company who already have eternal life (verses 2, 3), because they "received" and "believed" Christ's message (verse 8). They are hated by the world (verse 14) and definitely are not of the world (verse 16). He prayed for those who had believed, and for all "which shall believe on me through their word; That they all may be one . . . " (verses 20, 21). Any attempt on the part of men to create a superchurch organization of all religions on the basis of Christ's high-priestly prayer is a gross misuse and misinterpretation of that prayer. The unity our Lord speaks about in this chapter is based on a spiritual relationship created by the Holy Spirit in those men who have been born again (John 3:5, 7). In fact, it is wrong to try to bring about organic union between saved and unsaved persons. The Word of God says, "Be ye not unequally yoked together with unbelievers: for what fellowship hath righteousness with unrighteousness? and what communion hath light with darkness? And what concord hath Christ with Belial? or what part hath he that believeth with an infidel? And what agreement hath the temple of God with idols? for ye are the temple of the living God; as God hath said, I will dwell in them, and walk in them; and I will be their God, and they shall be my people. Wherefore come out from among them, and be ye separate, saith the Lord, and touch not the unclean thing; and I will receive you, And will be a Father unto you, and ye shall be my sons and daughters, saith the Lord Almighty" (II Corinthians 6:14-18).

I will not set myself up as a judge of the intentions and motives of those ecumenically minded religious leaders who are attempting to create a world church, nor will I question their sincerity. But I am unable with good conscience to approve or participate in the World Council program of trying to build "The coming Great Church" made up of all churches which have in them leaders who, by their own confession, through their spoken and written words, deny the essential doctrines of the historic Christian Faith as set forth in the New Testament, and that Jesus Christ is the one and only Saviour and Lord. There can never be organic union apart from doctrinal agreement and a true experiential knowledge of Christ. God's true Ecumenical Church is a union of all believers and a bulwark against all unbelief, even when that unbelief is in the heart of a man who is a leader in organized religion.

Dr. Henry P. Van Dusen in his book *World Christianity* says, "To an age destined to survive, if at all, as 'one world', we bring the beginnings of *a united church.*" If Dr. Van Dusen is speaking the mind of other leaders in the Ecumenical Movement, then it appears that one of the desired goals of a united World Church is that of survival. For quite some time there have been serious doubts that our civilization can survive many more generations. This fear has been spreading ever since the development of H-bombs of sufficient megaton power to wipe out our present civilization. To strive for world peace is a worthy and noble ambition, however every student of the Bible should know that a union of all religions is not the method by which peace can and will be achieved.

At the first Ecumenical Council in the city of Jerusalem in the first century the purposes of God were made crystal clear through the Apostle James. God is presently visiting nations through His Church, saving individuals regardless of nationality, race or color. Those who are being saved are at the same time being added to His Church (Acts 15:13, 14). James continues, "After this I (the Lord) will return, and will build again the tabernacle of David, which is fallen down . . . " (Acts 15:16, 17). *After what?* The answer is clear, namely, after God has taken out from among the nations a people for His name, which people make up His true Church. *After that* Christ will return and establish His kingdom of peace in the earth. The Church will never bring in Christ's kingdom, simply because this is not in God's plan and purpose for her. The kingdom cannot come until the King comes. So, then, let the Church be the Church and fulfill her mission of preaching the Gospel of Christ to the uttermost part of the earth.

The Development of the Superchurch

One views with interest the rapid development of this growing World Church. My itinerant ministry keeps me constantly on the move, and this affords an opportunity to observe ecumenical attitudes and activities in almost every part of our own country as well as in other countries.

The New York Times Service released a news item disclosing the fact that Union Theological Seminary and Fordham University have agreed to pool their professors, their credits and their library resources. "The agreement is said to be the first contractual sharing of graduate resources in theology between a Protestant and a Roman Catholic institution." The announcement of the agreement was made jointly by the Rev. Dr. John C. Bennett, president of Union Seminary, and the Rev. Leo McLaughlin, president of Fordham University. According to Dr. Bennett, "The program is in keeping with the whole modern ecumenical spirit of the Christian churches."

In Oberlin, Ohio, Protestant unity leaders moved closer to the spirit and pattern of the Vatican's Ecumenical Council as they sought paths of merger for six historically divided denominations. "Meeting on the campus of Oberlin College, representatives of the Episcopal, Methodist, Presbyterian, Evangelical United Brethren, the United Church of Christ, and the International Convention of Christian Churches (Disciples of Christ) listened without voicing objection to study commission reports that could shake the foundation of American Protestantism" *(The Detroit News)*.

Apparently the Oberlin meeting did not produce the desired results speedily enough to satisfy some of the leaders, because a later report released by the *New York Times Service* revealed a plan for uniting seven Protestant denominations with 23 million members within the next 5 to 13 years. The plan was drafted in Washington by a commission headed by the Rev. Dr. Eugene Carson Blake, the then newly elected general secretary of the World Council of Churches. Participants in this consultation are the Protestant Episcopal Church, the United Presbyterian Church in the U. S. A., the Methodist Church, the United Church of Christ, the Evangelical United Brethren Church and the African Methodist Episcopal Church.

Canon Albert J. duBois, head of the 11,000 member American Church Union, the biggest unofficial Episcopal group in the world, predicted and encouraged a swing to the Catholic Church. He cited two trends: (1) A changing climate within the Roman Catholic Church that makes it more acceptable to other liturgical-minded Christians. (2) A growing appreciation in Episcopalian worship for "the full traditional and catholic emphasis."

For six consecutive weeks a Roman Catholic family attended the Episcopal Church of the Incarnation in Detroit, mistaking it for a Roman Catholic Church. The bulletin board outside the church posted a daily Mass, a Mass schedule for holy days, a time for the Rosary, and "confessions by appointment."

In Northeast Michigan, Protestant and Roman Catholic clergymen met "to chart a pathway to goodwill among members of various religious groups" through a "Christian Interfaith Clergy Conference." The keynote address was brought by a Baptist pastor followed by two more addresses from a Roman Catholic priest and a Presbyterian pastor.

In Philadelphia, some Roman Catholic and United Presbyterian leaders proposed a joint prayer book which they hoped would lead to joint worship by members of the two churches on special occasions, such as Thanksgiving Day. In San Francisco, Roman Catholic and Protestant churches meet annually for an "Ecumenical Hymn Sing." It is called an "Inter-faith Program." A committee has proposed the preparation of an inter-faith hymnal.

In Clinton, Iowa, there was standing room only as some 1,000 Protestants and Romanists gathered in the First United Presbyterian Church for a joint worship service. The sermon was delivered by Msgr. Ambrose J. Burke of St. Mary's Roman Catholic Church.

In Atlanta, Georgia, Roman priests were urged to become acquainted with clergy of other churches in the neighborhood and seek membership in ministerial associations.

Cardinal Cushing of Boston has approved the reading of the Revised Standard Version of the *Oxford Annotated Bible*. This means that Roman Catholics are free to use this edition in home Bible reading and study groups. It is of interest to note that Cardinal Cushing's approval is not given to a special Roman Catholic version of the Bible, but to an edition already in use by Protestants.

There seems to be no end to the ever growing mass of illustrative material which shows clearly the rapid development of the modern Ecumenical Movement. But before we conclude this part of our study, I feel that some attention should be given to the new relation between Judaism and Romanism.

In January, 1964, Pope Paul VI made history when he visited the Holy Land. This was the first visit of a Pope to Jordan and Israel. On New Year's Day the Pope said that he expected his pilgrimage to have tremendous impact for years to come. In preparation for the giant step of eventually bringing Judaism into the world's superchurch, the Vatican issued a statement absolving Jews of sole responsibility for the death of Christ. This softening up process was quite effective. It brought warm response from Rabbi Maurice N. Eisendrath, president of the Union of American Hebrew Congregations, who said, "We Jews have long clamored for this indispensable change in official Catholic dissemination of facts and interpretation. But how long can we Jews persist in ignoring Jesus? How long then before we can admit that His influence was a beneficial one — not only to the pagans but to the Jews of His time as well?"

We have glanced at but a few of the many developments which mark the advance of this modern ecumenical religion movement, most of which would have been deplored by Protestants, Jews and Romanists only a few years ago. But it is clear that efforts will increase in this direction, and that more and more we will witness mergers of religious groups in the days ahead.

The Delusion of the Superchurch

Dr. Herman A. Hoyt, president of Grace Theological Seminary, said, "The ecumenical situation today is accurately described as a jig-saw puzzle. Its vast dimensions, its multiplied details, its complex doctrines, its strange divisions, its subtle devices, its motivating dynamics, and its intertwining and interlocking relationships reach beyond that point where any unaided human being is quite able to comprehend the total situation. Apart from the floodlight of the Word of God the Ecumenical Movement would continue to remain a jig-saw puzzle."

In Edinburgh, criticism of the Ecumenical Movement aroused interest at the General Assembly of the Free Church of Scotland. The Assembly, which met simultaneously with the General Assembly of the larger Presbyterian Church of Scotland, was told by Professor R. A. Finlayson, vice-convenor of the committee on public questions, religion and morals, "We cannot regard the present Ecumenical Movement as a distinctively Christian movement at all. It is a political-ecclesiastical movement making a strong bid for political power and ready to jettison its faith and all Christianity in the attempt." He charged that the movement was rallying its forces to give the world the impression of unity and power, but that when the ecclesiastical machinery is complete, the state might well take it over, as it did in Nazi Germany.

The leaders in the modern Ecumenical Movement have been deluded in being sidetracked from the major function of Christ's true Church. Modern churchmen of ecumenical persuasion, along with Roman Catholic nuns, are working industriously in civil rights programs, labor unions, politics, industry, international problems and numerous other civic affairs, including agitation against America's participation in war. But in so doing they are meddling in affairs outside the domain and duty of Christ's Church. Our Lord never intended that His Church should play a heroic role in saving the world from its many ills. It is my personal opinion that this delusion of the National and World Council of Churches is a satanic substitute introduced in order that the real issue should be overshadowed by this parade of civil affairs. The program of the Ecumenical Movement is only remotely related to the real purpose for the true Church's existence. Its program has no message to the individual unsaved person who is sick with the malady of sin and perishing without Christ. Its program gives the impression that it is concerned exclusively with its own self-preservation guarding the vast amount of wealth in real estate, annuities, investments and preserving the jobs of the many thousands of "clergymen," some of whom fear the loss of their jobs. While every true Christian should be concerned about the social ills surrounding him, the major function of Christ's true Church is the proclamation of His saving Gospel to the uttermost part of the earth. And wherever Christ's Gospel is preached and believed, social conditions always improve.

In the modern Ecumenical Movement there is the growing tendency to downgrade the Bible as the inspired and infallible Word of God, resulting in a shift from the spiritual to the social. The New Testament record shows that the strength of the Early Church had been her reliance on the Scriptures as the inerrant Word of God and her obedience to them in matters of faith and practice. But the modern church movement is being dangerously deluded. People go to church on Sunday seeking to have their spiritual needs met. They want to know the mind of Christ, the "Thus saith the Lord." But because the minister has relegated the Bible to a lesser place (or no place at all), those needy souls, hungering for the Bread of God, must listen to twaddle about higher wages, disarmament, the nation's foreign policy, federal aid to education, civil rights, the admission of Red China to the United Nations, urban renewal, etc. Thus the blind are leading the blind.

The ecumenical soup being concocted by this modern movement neither smells good nor tastes good. Every cook knows you cannot add equal amounts of garlic and meat and come up with a dish that will be palatable and nourishing. Already the ecumenical leaders have tossed out so many vital and necessary ingredients so as to be left holding a pot of weak broth which contains no balm for sin-sick souls. The result is a creeping paralysis that is overcoming all denominations. This is a delusion of modern ecumenism.

Cardinal Alfredo Ottaviani received one of the greatest ovations ever given in a Vatican Council when he urged that the Council call governments to join in a single world republic to preserve peace. And yet he made no suggestion at all as to how the masses of people in the world could be reached with Christ's saving Gospel. This is a delusion of modern ecumenism.

On October 13, 1966, *The News-Sentinel* of Fort Wayne, Indiana carried two announcements of religious activity which relate to our study. One reads as follows, "The 'Friday Noon Men's Search Group' of the Crescent Avenue Evangelical United Brethren Church will have its first of six fall sessions. 'The Christian's Role in the Civil Rights Movement' will be the topic of the first session."

The second announced a meeting of the Indiana Council of Churches for the sole purpose of discussing the issues to come before the Indiana State Legislature in 1967. The issues were "mental health, repeal of capital punishment, corrections, civil and human rights, and social welfare." This is a satanic substitute for the preaching and teaching of God's Word. The Christian message, when preached and practiced, reduces mental disease, moral degeneracy, racial misunderstanding and poverty. The Indiana Council of Churches program is a delusion of modern ecumenism.

July 12-26, 1966, at the Ecumenical Center in Geneva, more than 400 delegates from 87 countries were gathered to conduct a world conference on church and society. The delegates present were invited by the World Council of Churches to examine once again that old question: What is the function of the church in solving social ills? Here were the experts in various fields, most of them "laymen," supposedly qualified to speak on the multiplicity of problems resulting from the collapse of nations, the rise of a new nationalism, the population explosion, nuclear power, space travel, antibiotics, the Asian military conflict and a host of other subjects. This conference had been four years in preparation, having been authorized by the Central Committee of the World Council of Churches in 1962. The main theme, "Christians in the Technical and Social Revolution of Our Time," was explored under a specific topic, namely, *the nature and function of the state in a revolutionary age.* While it is true that other topics were discussed, all were related to the idea of social responsibility of Christendom. And after all was said and done, the embarrassing fact remains that the Geneva conference neither discussed nor decided upon the Church's true mission, which is our Lord's Great Commission, "Go ye into all the world, and preach the gospel to every creature" (Mark 16:15). In my opinion, the Central Committee of the World Council of Churches, meeting at the Ecumenical Center in Geneva, deliberated and dismissed under a delusion.

Now I am aware of the fact that we Christians in the evangelical mainstream are being charged with isolation from the world which keeps us from considering and coping with its concerns. One ecumenical leader said that our program includes preaching and evangelism unrelated to social service. We are accused of not involving ourselves in the great social problems men are facing, such as racism, war, poverty, family disintegration, communism, mental disease, and the like. A well-known missionary-statesman said, "In Latin America today a whole generation is turning away from religion and the churches because religion as they have known it for centuries has been sublimely indifferent to many of the basic needs of people."

Because there might be some truth in the above charges does not make them altogether valid. To begin with, do the "churches" and the "religions" of the world, which make up the modern ecumenical movement, constitute Christ's true Church? Can we take a hodgepodge of doctrines, declarations, denials and disbeliefs, toss them into a common melting pot and call the ecumenical soup Christianity? Is there any Biblical justification for identifying this strange mixture with the New Testament Church? The answer is a clear and certain No! The early Christians were of one faith and doctrine, they surrendered to the Lordship of Jesus Christ and to the fact that He was the sovereign Head of His Church; they acknowledged one commission, namely, to proclaim salvation in Christ to the uttermost part of the earth. And I hasten to add without fear of contradiction that, wherever the pure Gospel of Christ has been preached, and the converts have been instructed in Christian living according to the New Testament epistles, social conditions improve; savages become civilized, the naked are clothed, hospitals are built, schools are constructed and modern means of agriculture are introduced. In the remotest jungles I have witnessed the healing of social ills, the fruit of the faithful preaching and teaching of the Word of God. The modern Ecumenical Movement has been deluded in the formation of its unbiblical personnel and program. The merging of all religions into one earth-wide ecclesiastical organization is not Christ's Church, nor is the ecumenical social gospel Christ's Gospel.

The Description of the Superchurch

Many church historians regard the dawn and development of the Ecumenical Movement to have ushered in what they themselves call "the ecumenical age." What they mean is a decisive period in human history in which Christendom attains full maturity, a time in which the church comes of age. As Dr. Carl H. F. Henry has said, "After a half-century of consolidation it breathes its own life, boasts a central committee of 100, a hierarchy with an enlarging bureaucracy, and a world headquarters in Geneva."

This is all very remarkable because the New Testament anticipates and describes just such a church. It is to an examination of the inerrant Biblical description of this superchurch that we will now give ourselves. This description as found in the prophetic Scriptures was believed in the Early Church and is being repudiated in the Modern Church. But God's record in His Word still stands and its clear fulfillment is before our eyes. Following is God's description of this religious monster of the end-time.

In Revelation 13 two beasts appear on the scene. The first is

seen rising out of the sea (13:1), and the second comes up out of
the earth (13:11). The first is the Antichrist who receives his
power and authority from the dragon (13:2).

At this point, three necessary and important observations should
not be overlooked: (1) This chapter has to do with *worship*.
Notice the frequent appearance of the word "worship" (13:4, 8,
12, 15). (2) The prophecies in this chapter will not reach their
final fulfillment until after Christ has taken His own church to
heaven. Here, then, is a post-rapture scene, a description of worship in the earth after every saved person has been raptured to
be with the Lord. (3) The devil is the person who is worshiped —
"and they worshipped the dragon which gave power unto the
beast . . ." (13:4). The "dragon" is clearly identified as "that old
serpent, called the Devil, and Satan, which deceiveth the whole
world . . ." (Revelation 12:9).

The passage shows plainly that this religious system is ecumenical (i.e., earth-wide) in its outreach. "*All* the world won-
dered after the beast" (13:3) ". . . *all* that dwell upon the earth
shall *worship* him" (13:8). These statements leave no doubt that
the whole inhabited earth is brought under one superchurch which
has as its head a man who is controlled by Satan himself. Actually
there is no choice for the people on earth to make, for no one
can say in that day, as is being said today, "Go to the church of your
choice." When this Ecumenical Movement reaches its highest
organizational peak it will be the only church on earth recognized
by world governments. At that time none of its members will be
saved because its worshipers are those dwelling upon the earth
"whose names are not written in the book of life of the Lamb slain
from the foundation of the world" (13:8). The truly saved ones,
who make up Christ's Church, will be in heaven and will be a
target of the Antichrist's blasphemous attacks (13:6).

The head of the world superchurch is described further by God
through the Apostle Paul when he writes about "that man of sin
. . . the son of perdition; Who opposeth and exalteth himself above
all that is called God, or that is worshipped; so that he as God
sitteth in the temple of God, shewing himself that he is God.
. . . Even him, whose coming is after the working of Satan with
all power and signs and lying wonders" (II Thessalonians 2:3, 4, 9).

This is the Antichrist, the first beast of Revelation 13, that Satan-controlled man of lawlessness who will deify himself and demand the worship of all his subjects on earth. I know that some of you are shocked to see this amazing revelation that the world's largest church is to be controlled by Satan, but this is actually the devil's ecumenical church.

Satan's chief business is religion. As a matter of fact it was his religion that made him the wicked deceiver that he is. God did not create Satan as he now is. Just as man is not now in the original state in which God created him, so Satan is not now what he was when God created him. God did not create man a sinner; man became a sinner. God did not create a spirit-being a devil; he became the devil. The account of the *when* and *how* of Satan's origin is recorded in Isaiah 14. In his original state, before he became the devil, this created angel's name was Lucifer (14:12). Read verses 13 and 14, mark the five "I wills," and you will know the reason for Lucifer's fall. *"I will* ascend into heaven, *I will* exalt my throne above the stars of God: *I will* sit also upon the mount of the congregation, in the sides of the north: *I will* ascend above the heights of the clouds; *I will* be like the most High." In his last "I will" one sees the height of wickedness and folly, namely, that any creature should think that he can dethrone his creator and enthrone himself.

But why did Satan attempt to dethrone God and usurp the throne of God? The Bible has the answer! You will find it in the story of Christ's temptation recorded in Matthew 4 and Luke 4. From a high mountain the devil showed our Lord the kingdoms of this world and then said to Him, "All these things will I give thee, if thou wilt fall down and *worship* me" (Matthew 4:9; Luke 4:7). There you have it! The one thing the devil wanted was *worship*, and that ever has been and still is his ambition. The great contest today is over the worship of man. God wants the worship of man and the devil seeks to be worshiped by man. And it is clear that the modern Ecumenical Movement is the devil's superchurch through which he is achieving his goal, and which will be finalized after the Rapture of Christ's Church and the Man of Sin is revealed. The Apostle Paul wrote, "But if our gospel be hid, it is hid to them that are lost: In whom the god of this world hath blinded the minds of them which believe not, lest the light of the glorious gospel of Christ, who is the image of God, should shine unto them" (II Corinthians 4:3, 4). "For such are false apostles, deceitful workers, transforming themselves into the apostles of Christ. And no marvel; for Satan himself is transformed into an angel of light. Therefore it is no great thing if his ministers also be transformed as the ministers of righteousness; whose end shall be according to their works" (II Corinthians 11:13-15). This is precisely what our Lord predicted would happen in Christendom when, in His parabolic teaching, He said that the devil would sow his tares among the wheat, that is, the children of Christ's kingdom would find the children of the wicked one in their very midst (Matthew 13:24, 25, 36-43).

Today we see this strange mixture in the modern Ecumenical Movement. No one will deny that there are saved men in the World Council of Churches, men of ecumenical persuasion. But we know for certain that, when our Lord comes in the air to catch up His own, these saved men will be removed from the devil's ecumenical church. Imagine, if you can, the world's superchurch, immediately after the rapture of the true Church, not having one saved person in it! This is God's description of the modern Ecumenical Movement, the coming World Church.

The Domain of the Superchurch

The Ecumenical Church is manifestly displaying its power and influence with remarkable progression. At the turn of the century few persons, except those who studied the prophetic Scriptures, could have envisioned what is taking place in the world today. But we know that the ever-growing influence of the ecumenical situation is gradually fulfilling the Bible's prediction.

In Revelation 17 there is a somewhat lengthy account of this religious monstrosity. It is symbolized by a woman called "the great whore" (17:1) or "harlot" (ASV). She is one of four women in Revelation all of whom symbolize religious worship of a kind. Jezebel (2:20) represents pagan idolatry; the woman clothed with the sun (12:1) is Israel; the Lamb's wife (19:7) is Christ's true Church; and the whore in chapter 17 is the World Church in the time of the end.

The domain of this superchurch is suggested first by the word "great" (17:1), referring to power, position, prominence, describing the size of this tremendous system that has developed through the years until it has reached gigantic proportions.

She is designated further as "the great whore that sitteth upon many waters" (17:1). This same chapter gives the interpretation of the "waters." "The waters which thou sawest, where the whore sitteth, are peoples, and multitudes, and nations, and tongues" (17:15). The symbolism represents a world organization with an influence that has spread to every land and people of all languages, and it means that her authority has penetrated to the remotest part of the earth. This is the last great religious system in the earth embracing every known false religion.

"With whom the kings of the earth have committed fornication . . ." (17:2). The power and persuasiveness of the whore are so compelling as to make her irresistible to the world's political powers. As in past history, so now in the end time, there is such a resurgence of religious power and influence over the state that governments find it impossible not to acquiesce. They feel that some sort of union with religion is necessary if they are to hold the allegiance of their people.

The absoluteness of her domain is seen in the words, "and I saw a woman sit upon a scarlet coloured beast . . ." (17:3). This beast is the same personality of Revelation 13:1, the Antichrist and final ruler of the world before Christ comes. The ten horns are ten kings (17:12) comprising the federation which becomes the final end-time power. The whore rides the beast, showing her control over this organization of nations. And even though they hate her (17:16), they do for a time bow the knee to her false religious system. The world saw a sample of this in October, 1965, when the United Nations extended the extraordinary "courtesy" to Pope Paul VI, Christendom's most eminent spokesman for ecumenism, to address them. This is the forerunner of a soon coming event when the world's great religious system will dominate the political power.

Now we know that this is an unholy alliance, called "fornication" (17:2). Actually the Ecumenical Movement is prostituting religion in order to achieve power. That is why God calls her the "whore" or "harlot." A harlot, in the normal use of the term, is a woman who misuses the function of sex. Every misuse of sex is selfish. Every harlot who cohabits with men, other than the one to whom she is lawfully married, destroys the divine purpose for sex. This produces illegitimate offspring, a mixture that can result only in confusion and degeneration. God calls her "the mother of harlots and abominations of the earth" (17:5). As the "mother of harlots" she is the original source of this evil, mothering a whole brood of harlots. Dr. Hoyt says, "There is one great overall false church or system of religion, yet there are many segments of this great system as indicated by the many harlots who are her children. Associated with these harlots are the multitude of abominations, the vile and loathsome practices, the false doctrines, the pagan rites, the hideous perversions that likewise trace their origins to her. Early in the course of the human race Satan counterfeited true religion with paganism. This counterfeit finally reaches its fulness in the false religious system at the end of the age, gathering up at last all segments of false worship under one head."

"And the woman was arrayed in purple and scarlet colour, and decked with gold and precious stones and pearls, having a golden cup in her hands full of abominations and filthiness of her fornication" (17:4). Her dominion is characterized also by her wealth. Here we see both her royalty and her riches. She is "arrayed in purple" and holds vast stores of treasure in her possession. Any person who travels can see this vast wealth in the shrines, altars, "sacred" places, church buildings, hospitals, schools, colleges, universities, convents, seminaries, and large investments in banking, oil and liquor industries.

Indeed, religion is big business. And one day, in the not too distant future, the sum total of religious wealth will be in the common treasury of the World Church. Little wonder the kings of the earth are flirting with the harlot. They see her hundreds of millions of members representing numerical strength, and billions of dollars which is a large percentage of the world's wealth.

The Destruction of the Superchurch

The prophetic Scriptures present a picturesque description of the future of the World Church, and the apocalyptic outlook is not at all promising. In spite of her strength and influence she is doomed.

The *instrument* in her destruction is the Beast and the ten kings who have come to world power. "And the ten horns which thou sawest upon the beast, these shall hate the whore, and shall make her desolate and naked, and shall eat her flesh, and burn her with fire" (17:16). During the first three and one half years of the Tribulation the world powers unwillingly submit to the control of the Ecumenical Church. But they submit, nevertheless, in order that they might achieve their ultimate goal of world power (17:12, 13). The reasons why they recognize and receive her are obvious; her influence is irresistible so that they become susceptible to her power, her prostitution, her possessions and prestige. But now they loath her with disgust.

The *inspiration* to destroy her comes ultimately from God Himself, "For God hath put it in their hearts to fulfil his will" (17:17). While it is true that the nations never did have respect for this huge system of organized religion, verse 17 reminds us that God is upon His throne and that He is the almighty Sovereign over His universe, directing the course of events. As in times past, so once again God makes the wrath of man to praise Him (Psalm 76:10). He "worketh all things after the counsel of his own will" (Ephesians 1:11). Those united nations, believing that absolute power is in their hands, refuse longer to submit to the woman's control. They have used her to satisfy their lust for power, and now they conclude that they no longer need her.

The *interference* of God in the affairs of the World Church is most assuredly justified as are all His acts. The Biblical description of this religious monster demands that she be divinely judged. One of the great deceptions has been that everything religious is right. In fact, there are laws to protect persons on the basis of their religious convictions. But God's thoughts are not man's thoughts. There are reportedly more than four hundred different religions in the United States ranging from the death of God movement to that of finding God through LSD. Be sure that the day of divine reckoning will come. This religious freak, made up of all the world's religions, must come to nought. God has a plan for His church, for Israel and for the nations of the world, and "the words of God shall be fulfilled" (Revelation 17:17).

The *intensity* of her destruction is described in verse 16. The united political power shall make her "desolate." "In one hour she is made desolate" (Revelation 18:19). There is a common Greek root in our two English words "desolate" and "widow." A widow is a woman for whom support has been withdrawn. Paul uses the two words together when he writes, "a *widow* indeed and *desolate*" (I Timothy 5:5). At the height of the superchurch's career she boasted, "I sit a queen, and am no widow, and shall see no sorrow" (Revelation 18:7). But her day of sorrow will surely come, that day when all State and Federal aid will be withdrawn, including political, financial and military aid. She will come to nought. Paul uses the same word to describe Sarah when Abraham turned from her because of her barrenness (Galatians 4:27).

The prophecy states further that she shall be made "naked" (Revelation 17:16). A naked person is one divested of clothing. The word "naked" is the Greek word *gumnos* from which our word "gymnast" is derived. The gymnast removes all unnecessary clothing, thereby leaving off the outer garments of beauty and finery which attract. In verse 4 we read that "the woman was arrayed in purple and scarlet colour, and decked with gold and precious stones and pearls . . . ." But the day will come when she will appear before the eyes of all in her true character, a shameless and abandoned woman. Our Lord says to her, "Thou sayest, I am rich, and increased with goods, and have need of nothing; and knowest not that thou art wretched, and miserable, and poor, and blind, and *naked*" (Revelation 3:17). And now before it is too late He tenderly appeals, "I counsel thee to buy of me gold tried in the fire, that thou mayest be rich; and white raiment, that thou mayest be clothed, and that the shame of thy nakedness do not appear; and anoint thine eyes with eyesalve, that thou mayest see" (3:18).

But the prospects of her heeding Christ's invitation are not bright. The ten kings shall *"eat her flesh,"* a term used to describe the action of the political powers when they devour the abundance of her wealth and influence. They shall *"burn her with fire,"* meaning, I take it, that they shall utterly destroy her as a fire would level a building. Her sacred buildings, idols, shrines, altars and magnificent temples will be reduced to rubble. This is "the judgment of the great whore" (17:1). "Babylon the great is fallen, is fallen . . ." (18:2). "For true and righteous are His (God's) judgments: for he hath judged the great whore, which did corrupt the earth with her fornication, and hath avenged the blood of his servants at her hand" (19:2).

And now I trust that my Christian readers will be conscious of the purposes of predictive prophecy, namely, to produce a spiritual and moral response in the people of God, to give light in this dark world for those well-meaning Christians who are caught in the net of this religious monster, and to quicken saving faith in the hearts of those who have not yet been born again.

It is with mixed emotions that I have written this chapter. There are ministers whom I have known and respected for many years, men who believe as I believe in matters of doctrine, but with whom I must disagree as to their associations with denominations which are affiliated with the National and World Councils of Churches and which are looking with favor upon the modern Ecumenical Movement. I must remind them once again that the cause for which they are working is already lost. The Bible states plainly that Satan's superchurch is doomed to collapse.

The *imperative* in view of her destruction is clear. "Come out of her, my people, that ye be not partakers of her sins, and that ye receive not of her plagues" (18:4). This command to separation is a Biblical one which is applicable at all times. It is a divinely-given imperative. Babylon will appear to compromise a little here and a little there, but in her basic beliefs and goals she will never change. So let every real believer who is a part of this horrible system make a complete severance. Will you heed the call of the Lord and come out of her?

And to any who read these lines not having been born again, will you not receive the Lord Jesus Christ now? For you He died, and for you He waits patiently now in order that you might be saved.

Chapter 2

The Coming Man of Sin

The expression "man of sin" appears once in Scripture in the King James Version (II Thessalonians 2:3). The setting in which Paul uses it is a prophetic scene which points to a time immediately preceding the Second Coming of Jesus Christ to the earth. This entire second chapter of II Thessalonians is one of the outstanding prophetic chapters in the Bible. It is unique in some of the points of revelation discussed, one of these being that "man of sin."

The Description of the Man of Sin

It might help somewhat at the outset if we can identify the "man of sin" as to a principle or a person. Is Paul speaking here merely of an anti-Christian principle, an evil influence to pervade the world prior to Christ's return? The word "man" *(anthropos)*, is not used elsewhere of other than a human being. Even though the phrase "man of sin" does describe a predominant characteristic such as is found in the expression "man of sorrows" (Isaiah 53:3), it can be identified with a particular person. None of us will deny that the "man of sorrows" is Jesus Christ.

33

Moreover, the use of the article in the designation *"the* man of sin," *"the* son of perdition," *"the* wicked (one)," lends support to the idea that an individual person is meant. Then, too, the use of the personal pronouns "himself" and "he" indicate a person (II Thessalonians 2:3, 4, 8).

Included with the fact that Paul gives to the "man of sin" names which can be applied to a person only, Daniel likewise speaks of him as a person. He is the king who raises his voice against the most High and opposes the saints (Daniel 7:24-26). He shall persecute, prosper for a season, and proudly boast in himself until his sudden end (Daniel 8:23-25). He is the deceiver, desolator and devastator of the end time (Daniel 9:27). He shall do what he will, say what he will, and declare war on all who oppose him, Palestine being one of his targets, where he himself is finally defeated (Daniel 11:36, 38, 41, 45). These descriptions and actions would not make sense if they were not attributed to a person.

Our Lord said, "I am come in my Father's name, and ye receive me not: if another shall come in his own name, him ye will receive" (John 5:43). We know that this prophecy was fulfilled in part over and over again. False christs and false messiahs have appeared from time to time since our Lord was upon the earth. But it has a final fulfillment yet future, for here Christ speaks of *"the* man of sin," the final attempt of man to impersonate God.

While we have before us this word of Jesus in John 5:43, let me suggest that there is a possible hint here that the "man of sin" will be a Jew. It is unlikely that the Jews will acclaim as their Messiah a man who is not of their own race. It is to the Jews that he will present himself as their protector and benefactor. "He shall confirm the covenant with many for one week" (Daniel 9:27). It is likely that he will encourage and even assist the Jews in the reconstruction of the Temple and the reestablishing of their sacrificial system. The reconstructed Temple at Jerusalem is possibly the one the "man of sin" occupies in II Thessalonians 2:4. An analysis of Daniel 11:37 would seem to indicate also that he will be a Jew, "Neither shall he regard the God of his fathers. . . ."

Some manuscripts favor "man of lawlessness" in the place of *man of sin.* Lawlessness is a form of sin, for "sin is lawlessness" (I John 3:4). It would seem, however, that the word *lawlessness* is the better word here. Lawlessness is disregard for law, any law, God's or man's. It is rebellion against law. Even though history shows us, as well as our own experience, that the principle of lawlessness is always present in the human race, the idea here is that lawlessness will reach its peak when it finally becomes embodied in the "man of lawlessness." The principle of lawlessness in his precursors must not be confused with the "man of sin" himself.

However, coming events cast their shadows before. There is no need to pile up statistics, or to give voluminous quotations to show that lawlessness is on the increase. The criminal courts throughout the world cannot keep up with this growing problem. The past twenty-five years have produced a growing revolt on the part of mankind against all laws that are binding upon any decent society. If this tendency to lawlessness increases as rapidly in the next quarter century as it has in the one through which we just passed, we are indeed fast approaching the end of the age and the Rapture of the Church. René Pache wrote in 1955, "Now in all domains today anarchy reigns: in art, in music, in painting, in literature, in morals, in education, in politics, as well as in religion. On every line, a complete disorder characterizes our era."

The description of the "man of sin" continues in the phrase, the "son of perdition." This is not merely a term of description but one also of destiny. It is a general term for doom and disaster both temporal and eternal. The word "perdition" connotes the idea of *destruction*, as in I Thessalonians 5:3 and II Thessalonians 1:9. We are not to think of the destruction of being, but of well-being. The same words, "son of perdition," were used by our Lord of Judas (John 17:12) where they doubtless referred to the proper destiny of one who chooses to rebel against God and His laws, thereby choosing his own destiny, "that he might go to his own place" (Acts 1:25). Paul wrote elsewhere of "the enemies of the cross of Christ: whose end is destruction [perdition]" (Philippians 3:18, 19).

The Designation of the Man of Sin

There has been much speculation by Bible teachers in their endeavor to identify the "man of sin." Centuries ago there were those who held that Nero was he. During the reformation the Pope was considered to be the "man of sin," and since that time the speculation has run wild from the Pope to Mussolini to Hitler to Stalin.

If the Christians, from Nero's day to our own, had studied the Scriptures that deal with the "man of sin," they would have known that he would not be revealed until after the Rapture of the Church. Paul wrote, "Now we beseech you, brethren, by the coming of our Lord Jesus Christ, and by our gathering together unto him, That ye be not soon shaken in mind, or be troubled, neither by spirit, nor by word, nor by letter as from us, as that the day of Christ is at hand" (II Thessalonians 2:1, 2). Here we should observe a change made by the revisers in translating this paragraph. In verse 2, the Revised Standard Version reads, "the day of the Lord," in the place of the "day of Christ." This distinction makes a difference. The "day of Christ" is always imminent. It begins with the Rapture, therefore it may begin at any moment. It is the day described in I Thessalonians 4:13-18.

Before attempting an explanation of "the day of the Lord," we should acquaint ourselves with the error that Paul is attempting to correct here. The Thessalonian believers had been taught that the "day of the Lord is just at hand" (verse 2, RSV). Someone had told them that that day was present, that is, they were then living in it. The false teaching had come to them by "spirit" or by "word" or by "letter." If they claimed to receive this teaching from the Holy Spirit, Paul contradicts such a possibility. If they were told it orally or through a letter, Paul denies that he had anything to do with it. "Let no man deceive you," he writes. If such information was sent them in a letter, it was a forgery. If they were taught that they were in the "day of the Lord," they were deceived.

The "day of the Lord" is that period of time, commencing with the seventh week of Daniel and culminating at the judgment of the Great White Throne, when God will deal with sinners in judgment. Paul did not want the believers thrown off their equilibrium by the shocking untruth that that day was then present with them. The Apostle denounces any rumor that he had said the "day of the Lord" had already come, and assures them that it had not come. We need to guard against doctrinal error that menaces the heart and mind, for Satan has a way of throwing the saints off balance mentally by some disturbing statement that has not an element of truth in it.

Now he proceeds to tell them why that day of judgment could not have been present with them. "Let no man deceive you by any means: for that day shall not come, except there come a falling away first, and that man of sin be revealed, the son of perdition" (II Thessalonians 2:3). The necessary prelude to "the day of the Lord" is the apostasy and the revelation of the "man of sin.". Just as the first coming of Christ was preceded by a period of apostasy during the reign of Antiochus Epiphanes (who ruled from 175-164 B.C.), the forerunner of the "man of sin," so also the Second Coming of Christ to the earth will not occur until the final apostasy has taken place. Apostasy and leaders of apostasy have always been with us, but the last great apostasy will be embodied in the "man of sin." The appearing of the final apostasy and its leader must be "*first*," that is, before "the day of the Lord."

Further evidence is given to show that no man living in Paul's day, nor at any time since, could be *declared* to be the "man of sin." "And now ye know what withholdeth that he might be revealed in his time" (II Thessalonians 2:6). The "he" refers back to the "man of sin." The point being made here is that there is a power restraining the "man of sin," and will continue to restrain him, in order that he might be revealed in his appropriate season. His appearing is impossible at present because there is a restraining power. In verse 6 this power is referred to as neuter, or a thing; but in the verse following (verse 7), the power is regarded as a Person. Just as the power of lawlessness is wielded in the man of lawlessness, even so the power that restrains him is wielded by One greater than he.

Many explanations have been suggested in an endeavor to identify the restrainer. Some who held that Nero was the "man of sin," believed that Seneca, his tutor, was the restrainer. Another says the restrainer is Satan, and that he is holding back the full force of rebellion against God until he himself is ready to step in and take over. Then it has been popularly held by some that the Roman government and its policies constituted the restraining power. But none of these suggestions seem to stand up under examination.

Nero could not have been the "man of sin" nor Seneca the restrainer, else the Second Coming of Christ would have already occurred. Satan could not be the restrainer of evil, for he is never shown in the Bible in such a role, nor will he be taken away during the tribulation even when evil reaches its zenith. Moreover, the coming of the "man of sin" is said to be "after the working of Satan" (II Thessalonians 2:9). "And if Satan cast out Satan, he is divided against himself; how shall then his kingdom stand?" (Matthew 12:26). Human government cannot be the restrainer, for while the governments of men do restrain a certain amount of evil, there will be rigid governmental regulation during the Tribulation. Law enforcement agencies, both national and international, are at their wit's end. As soon as one evil contrivance is uncovered and dealt with, another appears. It is not possible that human legislation will ever fully restrain evil.

Who, then, is the Restrainer? Who is holding back the "man of sin" until that fit and destined moment comes? From my study of history, both secular and sacred, there has never been a power, apart from divine power, that could restrain evil. This is so from the very nature of the case. "The heart is deceitful above all things, and incurable. . . ." (Jeremiah 17:9, *J. N. Darby*). A man may rid himself of one evil, but unless Christ comes into that heart and takes over, seven other evils, worse than the one gotten rid of, will enter and dwell there (Matthew 12:43-45).

It seems unreasonable to assume that any power, apart from the power of God, can successfully restrain evil. In the days of Noah it was the Holy Spirit who restrained sin. God has said, "My Spirit shall not always strive with man" (Genesis 6:3). The Lord Jesus said that after His departure the Holy Spirit will come, and that "He will reprove the world of sin" (John 16:8). In this present age, which had its commencement at Pentecost in the fulfillment of Christ's promise to send the Holy Spirit (John 16:7), it is the Spirit who strives against sin. On the day of Pentecost the Spirit of God descended and filled the disciples (Acts 2:4). Then followed Peter's sermon in the Spirit's power which brought deep conviction and repentance of sin (Acts 2:37, 38). The Bible shows that from Genesis to this present hour the Holy Spirit has been the Restrainer against sin.

I conclude, therefore, that the most natural explanation of the Restrainer is arrived at by supernatural revelation, the Word of God itself. The Restrainer is the Holy Spirit. The Holy Spirit indwells the Church and by the Church I mean that corporate body made up of individual members. Each member of Christ's Church is indwelt by the Holy Spirit. "If any man have not the Spirit of Christ, he is none of his" (Romans 8:9). "Know ye not that ye are the temple of God, and that the Spirit of God dwelleth in you?" (I Corinthians 3:16). "What, know ye not that your body is the temple of the Holy Ghost which is in you, which ye have of God, and ye are not your own?" (I Corinthians 6:19). At the time of the Rapture which Paul describes in I Thessalonians 4:13-18, the Church and the Holy Spirit will be taken out of the world. The removal of the Spirit and the Church will release the world to unprecedented lawlessness.

This view is objected to on the grounds that it necessitates a change of the Spirit's mode of operation and that He leaves the world entirely. The objection is not valid, however, when we consider the Spirit's operation before Pentecost. Just as the Spirit operated in the world before Pentecost, coming upon men for special enduements to perform particular tasks, so He will operate after the Rapture. Dr. Walvoord writes, "It will mean a reversal of Pentecost. Just as the Spirit came on Pentecost, so He will leave when Christ takes the Church out of the world." None can deny that the presence of Spirit-filled and Spirit-directed believers in the world exerts an influence for good. Though true believers are in the minority in the world, they do restrain evil to some extent. Now picture, if you can, the world when all the saved people have been removed. Unsaved persons only will be left to run government, industry, religion and all other enterprises.

The conclusion of the matter, then, is that the Day of the Lord could not have come in Paul's day, because the Spirit and the Church had not been taken away and the "man of sin" had not been revealed. Therefore, any attempt to identify him with any person who lived since Paul's day is useless.

But who is the "man of sin"? Let us return to a statement made by our Lord in His high-priestly prayer. He said, "While I was with them in the world, I kept them in thy name; those that thou gavest me I have kept, and none of them is lost, but the son of perdition; that the scripture might be fulfilled" (John 17:12). Now turn to II Thessalonians 2:3, and you will have seen the only two passages in the Scripture where the name "son of perdition" is used. In the first instance it is applied to Judas Iscariot, and in the second it refers to the "man of sin." They are called by the same name. Who was Judas Iscariot? He was the "son of perdition." Judas Iscariot and the "man of sin" are one and the same person.

Judas was a man (Matthew 26:24), but he was more than a man. Jesus said to him, "Have not I chosen you twelve, and one of you is a devil?" (John 6:70). In Greek different words are used for "devil" and "demon." There are many demons but only one devil.

On the night of the Passover, Luke writes, "Then entered Satan into Judas surnamed Iscariot, being one of the twelve" (Luke 22:3). At that moment Satan took over the body of Judas, and Judas immediately went out joining himself with Christ's enemies to betray Him (verse 4). To the best of my knowledge this is the only passage where it is said that Satan entered into a man. There are recorded instances where demons entered the bodies of men and women, but never Satan himself, save this one instance.

That Judas was never saved is clear from another passage. When our Lord washed the feet of His disciples, an act symbolizing the removal of any defilement that might hinder their communion with Himself, He said, "Ye are clean, but *not all*" (John 13:10). Why did Christ say, "not all"? The Holy Spirit supplies the explanation in the words immediately following, "For he knew who should betray him; therefore said he, Ye are not all clean" (verse 11). Judas never was a child of God.

The Revelation speaks of "the beast that ascendeth out of the bottomless pit . . . and will go into perdition" (Revelation 11:7; 17:8, 11). Many commentators identify the "beast" with the "man of sin." But how did he get into the bottomless pit? The Scripture says that Judas went to "his own place" (Acts 1:25). It is said of the beast that he "was," that is, he was on the earth. Next we are told that he "is not," that is, he "is not" now on the earth. Of Enoch it is written that "he *was not;* for God took him" (Genesis 5:24), that is, he "was not" any longer on the earth. When John wrote the

Revelation the beast was not then on the earth, though he had been on it at one time. He is now in the bottomless pit, but will ascend out of it after the Church is removed. And then he will "go into perdition" (Revelation 17:8, 11). Judas Iscariot will be the "man of sin." As Christ, the Seed of the woman, is God incarnate, so Judas Iscariot, the seed of the serpent, is the devil incarnate (Genesis 3:15).

The Designs of the Man of Sin

That this evil person, who shall be revealed after the Church is caught away, has blasphemous designs is clearly stated. *"Who opposeth and exalteth himself above all that is called God, or that is worshipped; so that he as God sitteth in the temple of God, shewing himself that he is God"* (II Thessalonians 2:4).

The spirit of pride and self-esteem are so developed in him that he claims deity. He will not worship, but will himself demand to be worshiped. The Apostle said that the coming of the man of sin *"is after the working of Satan"* (II Thessalonians 2:9). Satan will be the instigator and energizer of his evil designs. He will be the "seed" of the serpent (Genesis 3:15). Impersonating the devil, he will have the same aspirations as did Lucifer, evil ambitions which caused the "son of the morning" to become the devil, when he said, "I will ascend into heaven, I will exalt my throne above the stars of God: I will sit also upon the mount of the congregation, in the sides of the north: I will ascend above the heights of the clouds; I will be like the most High" (Isaiah 14:12-14). The reason for his self-exaltation was that he might be worshiped. Satan said to Christ, "All these things will I give thee, if thou wilt fall down and worship me" (Matthew 4:9).

The language Paul uses to set forth the designs of the "man of sin" is similar to that used by Daniel in his description of the willful king (Daniel 8:25; 11:36, 37). For a man to deify himself and command worship was not strange to Daniel and the Jews in captivity. Nebuchadnezzar set up the golden image, representing himself, and then demanded that all people bow down and worship. Those who refused were to be thrown into the fiery furnace (Daniel 3:1-7). Revelation 13 is a prophecy of the rise and rule of the man of sin, of whom it is predicted, "All that dwell upon the earth shall worship him" (Revelation 13:8). Having others to worship him is not merely one of his designs but a demand as well.

His supreme sin will consist in this evil design to usurp the place of God. "He shall speak great words against the most High . . . and think to change times and laws [the laws of God]" (Daniel 7:25). But he will not be content with such an usurpation, he will succeed in having himself worshiped by all the inhabitants of the earth except those believers who are saved after the Rapture. This attempt to dethrone God and demand worship of himself will probably constitute the "abomination of desolation" prophesied by Daniel (9:27), and against which our Lord sounded a warning (Matthew 24:15).

René Pache in *The Return of Jesus Christ*, wrote,

> In our day we have witnessed the appearance of a movement of the godless in Russia. In 1928 it was said to have organized two hundred fifty thousand militants for the campaign against religion. There were ten thousand antireligious clubs. That same year there were at Leningrad seven hundred antireligious demonstrations. In three months, nine hundred churches were closed, and the newspaper, *The Godless*, brochures, and antireligious literature were published in millions of copies. This movement, having partially failed, seems for the moment to have diminished in violence. But prophecies allow us to foresee the time when it will lift its head anew and break forth on the entire world. In the hand of the Antichrist it will become a means of leveling all religions and of thus preparing for the worship of his own person.
>
> Once more let us look at that which is already happening around us. The cult of the superman toward which mankind marches is not new in itself. Often in the history of great potentates they have extracted from their subjects divine honors — for example, the Roman emperors. In our day they would force seventy million Japanese (and even Christians among them) to adore the Mikado and his ancestors. And it is incontestable that a dictator such as Hitler (to speak only of him) succeeded in creating around his person an entirely religious mysticism. He thus obtained from a large number of his subjects a consecration more total and a faith more absolute than that of many believers with reference to God.
>
> Moreover, the modern tendency is to deify not only certain men but the state itself. We have likewise seen how millions of persons very much "civilized" have come to worship their own nation (in short, to worship themselves), and to render worship to the all-powerful state. In the totalitarian regimes the latter has become a veritable Moloch which absorbs all of the living forces and

crushes all the individuals. A great German philosopher, Hegel, could write even a hundred years ago, "The individual exists only for the State. The state is divine, the absolute end, the 'true God,' the 'divine divinity' in itself which enjoys an authority and a majesty absolute."

Mussolini also encouraged a veritable worship of his person. The Fascist Grand Council wrote in a proclamation, "We have obeyed him, we obey him, and we shall obey him blindly in life and in death!" A Fascist journal wrote, "Our ideal cannot be the *God-man* [Jesus Christ], the God-man who loves and who suffers, the justified expiatory victim emerging against the background of the Apocalypse, of Gehenna and of Predestination. But it is the *Man-god* victorious, the hero of Hellenic myths, Mithras, the triumphant adversary of the Son and of the Bull; Siva, the god terrible and dancing, the cosmic beings powerful, brilliant, purified of passions, detached from desires, consecrated by mysteries. . . . Let us efface the Christian notion. We do not have the Semitic tradition imported from Palestine, but the Mediterranean tradition."

The Denial of the Man of Sin

It was given to the Apostle John alone to give to us a particular descriptive term as well as the denial of the "man of sin." The descriptive term is "the Antichrist" (I John 2:18, 22; 4:3; II John 7). The Apostle uses the expressions, "Antichrist," "many antichrists," "the Antichrist," "the spirit of Antichrist," (RSV). We proceed with our study on the assumption that "the man of sin" and "the Antichrist" are one and the same person.

The Apostle's first mention of the term is used in both the singular and plural — "antichrist . . . many antichrists" (2:18). As regards "antichrist," John says he "shall come." But he adds, "even now are there many antichrists." The former is the final personal Antichrist, and because it is "the last time," "the last hour," "the last days" (II Timothy 3:1), John reminds us that he is about to come. The many antichrists are but the forerunners of *the* Antichrist. This dispensation had just gotten under way in John's time. But now with 1900 years of church history behind us, it is obvious that antichrists have increased in number, and we may be certain, even though our Lord said that neither men nor angels would know the exact "hour" of His coming (Matthew 24:36), that the "last hour," or the last period to precede the return of our Lord Jesus Christ, is running out. The "last time" is the day of Christ.

The meaning of the word "antichrist" is necessary to a clearer understanding of his doctrine. The prefix "anti" suggests the two ideas of "opposed to" and "instead of." The Antichrist defies Christ and denies that He is the Christ of God. He is against Christ. "Who is a liar but he that denieth that Jesus is the Christ? He is antichrist, that denieth the Father and the Son" (I John 2:22). The definite article appears before the word "liar," so as to read, "Who is *the* liar?" The Antichrist impersonates all that is false. To deny that Jesus is the Christ is a lie, and he who instigates the denial is the father of the lie. The word "Christ" means "the anointed One," "the Messiah." The doctrine of the Antichrist, then, is a denial of this essential and eternal unity.

While *the* Antichrist is in view here, anyone who denies that Jesus is the Christ, the eternal Son and Anointed of the Father, is a representative of the ilk that the Antichrist will be. The tragedy is that many of the advocates of the system which denies Christ's deity, virgin birth, substitutionary atonement, bodily resurrection and coming again were once numbered among the company of professed believers. They took solemn vows to uphold and preach the doctrine they now deny. They once gathered at the communion table with the children of God and confessed to be one with them. John says, "They went out from us, but they were not of us; for if they had been of us, they would no doubt have continued with us: but they went out, that they might be made manifest that they were not all of us" (I John 2:19). The truly saved person has an "unction" (2:20), an anointing from the Holy Spirit. It is our baptism into the body of Christ (I Corinthians 12:13).

Along with the unction for *belonging,* there is the unction for *knowing.* "But ye have an unction from the Holy One, and ye know all things" (I John 2:20)! This may sound at first like an extravagant statement, "ye know all things," but considered in its context, it is understandable. The Apostle is contrasting the "truth" with a "lie," and he identifies the lie as that denial of the deity of our Lord Jesus Christ, and the "liar" as the one making the denial (verses 21, 22). But the child of God has dwelling in him the One who knows all things. Even the babe in Christ has the witness of the Holy Spirit in him, and thus he knows who Jesus is. The Christian possesses the true knowledge of Christ, while antichrists deny Him. The believer may not be capable of explaining the theological and doctrinal teachings about Christ, but he knows Christ experientially and what the Saviour has done for him, therefore he could never deny Him. Any religion that denies the above truth is antichristian in nature, and its doctrine is the doctrine of the Antichrist.

The fact is further emphasized in chapter four, "And every spirit that confesseth not that Jesus Christ is come in the flesh is not of God: and this is that spirit of antichrist, whereof ye have heard that it should come; and even now already is it in the world" (I John 4:3). Guy H. King has an interesting comment on verse 2 which has helped me to appreciate my Lord more. The verse reads, "Every spirit that confesseth that Jesus Christ is come in the flesh is of God." King says,

> For many years this passage troubled me, because I could not see why such tremendous issues should hang upon so simple a thing as the acknowledgment that JESUS CHRIST was an historical personage. Of course He was: even these false spirits will agree to that. Secular historians, quite independently of the Bible — Josephus, Pliny, for instance — record the fact. At last I thought I saw my way out — if only it were justifiable to translate the Greek differently from the Authorised Version by placing the little "is" in another position. Was I right? Some time back, I came into touch with a profound Greek scholar, and to my great glee, he said that my rendering of the original was perfectly allowable.
>
> Before giving you my conviction, let me remind you that "JESUS" is the Name of the Master's Humanity, and that "CHRIST" is the title of His Deity, the Divine anointed One come to be the promised and predicted Messiah, Saviour, and King. Do you see now what I am driving at? Yes; this is the suggested translation, "Every spirit that confesseth that JESUS IS CHRIST come in the flesh. . . ." An acknowledgment, you see, of His Deity. Chapter V:1 of the Epistle supports my interpretation, doesn't it? And the first and fundamental test of every spirit claiming to be of GOD is, "What think ye of CHRIST?" (Matthew 22:42).

Now look again at verse 3, "And every spirit that confesseth not that Jesus [is] Christ come in the flesh is not of God: and this is that spirit of [the] Antichrist. . . ." Inasmuch as the Antichrist is against Christ, he will deny the truth relating to Jesus, namely, that He is the Christ. Antichrist does not deny the historical man, Jesus of Nazareth, but he does deny that Jesus is the Messiah.

We live in a perilous day. What has been foretold as characteristic of the "last hour" may be seen clearly in our own day. Do not think for a moment that the warnings sounded here against Antichrist can be pushed into the future. "Even now are there antichrists . . . and even now already is it in the world." It is proved to be so by the prevalence of new thought, a new evangelicalism. Yesterday some of them were among us and seemingly one with us. Today they are denying the essential truths of our historic Christian faith. Modernism has taken over in some of our large denominations and Christ is denied.

"For many deceivers are entered into the world, who confess not that Jesus Christ is come in the flesh. This is a deceiver and an antichrist" (II John 7). If ever there was cause for believers to band themselves together in love for one another, we have one here. Many deceivers are roving about, leading into error. Their chief denial is that "Jesus [is] Christ come in the flesh." This is the antichristian system, the forerunner of *the* Antichrist. It denies the incarnation of God the eternal Son in the Person of Jesus of Nazareth. This error is easily identified. When a man denies that the human Jesus is the divine Christ, he is an antichrist in that he is a part of the antichristian system.

The Dominion of the Man of Sin

The apostasy in the earth will have its final consummation in the "man of sin" who will attain universal dominion. We recall that Satan offered to Jesus Christ all the kingdoms of the world. "Again, the devil taketh him up into an exceeding high mountain, and sheweth him all the kingdoms of the world, and the glory of them; And saith unto him, All these things will I give thee, if thou wilt fall down and worship me" (Matthew 4:8, 9). If anyone questions how Satan obtained the scepter of government in the earth, let him read again the story of the fall of our first parents. It will be remembered that dominion of the earth was given to Adam. "So God created man in his own image, in the image of God created he him; male and female created he them. And God blessed them, and God said unto them, Be fruitful, and multiply, and replenish the earth, and subdue it: and have dominion over the fish of the sea, and over the fowl of the air, and over every living thing that moveth upon the earth" (Genesis 1:27, 28). But in Genesis 3 dominion in the earth is transferred from Adam to Satan by right of conquest. On at least three occasions our Lord referred to Satan as "the prince of this world" (John 12:31; 14:30; 16:11). Thus the believer's conflict is said to be "against the rulers of the darkness of this world" (Ephesians 6:12). Satan is the directing head or governmental chief of this world system. "The whole world lieth in wickedness [the wicked one]" (I John 5:19).

It has been intimated by some that Satan was in charge of the earth when God originally created it, and that it was then he said in his heart, "I will ascend into heaven, I will exalt my throne above the stars of God [that is, above other ruling powers]: I will sit also upon the mount of the congregation, in the sides of the north: I will ascend above the heights of the clouds; I will be like the most High" (Isaiah 14:13, 14). For this presumptuous act God brought judgment upon this Adamite earth. That something had gone wrong in the created earth before Adam and Eve is evident from a careful reading of Genesis 1:2. There are competent Hebrew scholars who render the opening words of this verse, "And the earth *became* a desolation and ruin." Some professing Christians seize upon the King James Version, "the earth *was* without form," to support the "primeval ooze" theory. God did not create a chaos, or a desolation (Isaiah 45:18). Chaos is the result of divine judgment because of the failure of earth's first custodian.

In Luke's account of our Lord's temptation, Satan says, "All this power will I give thee, and the glory of them: for *that is delivered unto me;* and to whomsoever I will give it" (Luke 4:6). It was no idle word that Satan uttered when he said to Christ, "for that is delivered unto me." They were delivered to him, but not by God. It was man who relinquished his dominion and delivered it to Satan. Now if Christ would have surrendered to Satan and become his subject and worshiper, Satan would have turned over to Him the rule of this world. But such a rule would have to be under Satan's direction.

The "man of sin" will accept this offer. He will give himself completely to the devil and receive from the devil his power and authority, "whose coming is after the working of Satan with all power and signs and lying wonders" (II Thessalonians 2:9). "The dragon gave him his power" (Revelation 13:2). The power of "the man of sin" will be of supernatural origin which will account for his remarkable feats. "Power *was given* unto him to continue forty and two months" (Revelation 13:5). "Power *was given* him over all kindreds, and tongues, and nations" (Revelation 13:7). The supremacy of the "man of sin" cannot be explained by his unusual personality, but by an invisible supernatural power received from the devil. In the "man of sin" Satan finds one who will willingly accept his offer.

There are those who doubt that a world government is possible. But students of the Bible know that it must come. In 1950 Dr. Wilbur M. Smith wrote,

> During THE LAST FIVE YEARS hardly any issue of a great newspaper appears, almost never an issue of the *Congressional Record* is published, seldom any number of an outstanding serious periodical issues from the press, or a noteworthy book dealing with contemporary problems, but that, again and again, scores, hundreds, and thousands of times, we come upon the statement, arrived at by one path or another, that the only hope for humanity in this hour is a world federation, a *world government*.

One of the conditions of life to mark the end of the age, and one that will embrace the whole fabric of society, is the readiness to accept the leadership of any man who will, in the minds of the members of that society, meet certain qualifications. Plato's *Republic* purposes such a government, so that we can say the idea is not one of recent origin. Smith, quoting Immanuel Kant's *Toward Universal Peace*, tells us that Kant's idea was "a society of nations which would ostensibly embrace all nations of the earth. However visionary this ideal may appear to be, it is, nevertheless, the inevitable issue of the necessity in which men involve one another." World leagues and world federations have arisen in our day. Two of these, well-known, are the League of Nations and the United Nations. More recently the idea of a one world government has been imbibed by some ecclesiastical bodies. This idea will develop and meet with favor gradually as the age draws to a close, so that after the Church has been raptured, the world will be ready to accept the "man of sin."

Someone might ask in what part of the world the "man of sin" will appear first. At the outset his power will be manifested in the countries of the last kingdom of Nebuchadnezzar's dream image.

He will arise in the revived ancient Roman Empire. The first empire in Daniel's prophecy is Babylon (Daniel 2:31, 32, 38, 39). The second empire, represented by the breast and arms of silver (2:32), is that of the Medes and Persians (5:28-31), represented also by the bear (7:5) and by the ram (8:3). The third empire, represented by the belly and thighs of brass (2:32), is Greece (8:21), represented also by the winged leopard (7:6) and the goat (8:5). The fourth empire, represented by legs of iron, and feet part of iron and part clay (2:33), and by the fourth beast of 7:2-7, 23 is Rome. We know that in history Rome succeeded Greece. It is from the midst of the reconstructed fourth empire that the "man of sin," the great prince, shall arise (7:23-25). Compare Daniel 7:4-7 with Revelation 13:1, 2, and these indications will be confirmed. The seven heads are seven hills on which Rome was located at the time the Apostle John wrote (Revelation 17:7, 9, 18).

His dominion will not be confined, however, to the reconstructed Roman Empire. He will attain universal dominion. A number of men in the past have aspired to world supremacy. To mention a few there were Alexander, Caesar, Napoleon, Mussolini and Hitler. Let him who doubts that world domination by one man is not possible think of what might have happened if Germany had been first to discover the atom bomb during Hitler's rule. But God saw to it that no demon-possessed mad man could control such power before the appointed time. The world is now small enough for one man or one single power to conquer it. The late Dr. Albert Einstein said, "The secret of the bomb should be committed to a World Government. The World Government should have power over all military matters."

That the "man of sin" will realize universal dominion is clear from certain Scriptures. "The fourth beast shall be the fourth kingdom upon earth, which shall be diverse from all kingdoms, and shall devour *the whole earth,* and shall tread it down, and break it in pieces" (Daniel 7:23). ". . . *And power was given him over all kindreds, and tongues, and nations.* And all that dwell upon the earth shall worship him. . . ." (Revelation 13:7, 8). His dictatorship will be a totalitarian regime politically (Revelation 13:4, 7), religiously (II Thessalonians 2:4; Revelation 13:8, 15), and economically (Revelation 13:16, 17). Under such rule any who defy his dictates will have no right to exist. They will not be permitted to buy or sell since absolute control will be exercised over every piece of merchandise including food and clothing as well as employment.

The identification of those who submit to the "man of sin" is the number 666. "And that no man might buy or sell, save he that had the mark, or the name of the beast, or the number of his name. Here is wisdom. Let him that hath understanding count the number of the beast: for it is the number of a man; and his number is six hundred threescore and six" (Revelation 13:17, 18). I feel that I can offer no comments that would compare with those Dr. Pache has given to us. Therefore I quote his text in full.

> Much has been written on this passage and a thousand contradictory interpretations have been brought forth. We do not intend to give one more. However, certain indications could be useful. John says, "Let him who has intelligence calculate the number of the beast." In Greek (as in Hebrew and in Latin) the letters of the alphabet serve likewise as signs for the figures. *Alpha* signifies one; *beta,* two, etc. For any name it is, therefore, possible to add together the numerical value of each letter and to arrive at a total which forms the "number of a man." The name of the Antichrist will give the total of 666. Men have sought to apply this method with reference to all the persons in history who have seemed to be the Antichrist. By more or less arranging the letters of the titles of these persons they have arrived at the number 666 for the names of Nero, Mohammed, the pope, Napoleon, and even Hitler, not to speak of many others. In our opinion the proof that these interpretations are still premature is that they are all contradictory. . . . But there is another means, equally just, it seems to us, of understanding the famous number 666. We made allusion to it just now when comparing Christ with Antichrist. John says that the number 666 is a number of a man. It is evident that in the Apocalypse there are symbolic numbers. The number 7, for example, expresses fullness or perfection, and it is most often used with reference to God and Jesus Christ: the Lamb slain has seven horns and seven eyes which are the seven spirits of God (Revelation 5:6). On the other hand, the number 6 and its components refer to everything that is human: the 24 elders (Revelation 4:4); the 12 tribes of Israel, the 12,000, the 144,000 (Revelation 7:4-8). Six is the imperfect number par excellence, always below 7, the number of perfection. The Antichrist in his wrath will be able to raise himself and puff himself up beyond measure, extending his conquest even to the earth, causing himself to be worshipped even as if he were God. Everything that he makes will remain marked with the seal of fundamental imper-

fection and impotence: his number is and will remain the number of man three times repeated 6-6-6.

The Duration of the Man of Sin

The duration of his rule is brief. We have noted that he will not be revealed until after the Church and the Holy Spirit are removed from the earth. The rapture will bring to a close the present dispensation of the Church, and it will commence the seventieth "week" of Daniel's prophecy (Daniel 9). The "week" is equal to seven years, after which time Christ returns to the earth with His saints, so that the rule of the "man of sin" will not exceed seven years.

The duration of his rule is fixed beforehand by God. This seems to be indicated in several statements in Daniel: "The same horn made war with the saints, and prevailed against them; *Until* the Ancient of days came. . . . For at *the time appointed* the end shall be. . . . He shall prosper until the indignation be accomplished. . . ." God has set the bounds. The "man of sin" can go so far and no farther.

Though the time period seems of short duration, we may be certain that all of God's declared purposes for that period will be fulfilled. Actually the major fulfillment will take place during the last half of the "week," or three and one-half years. This is the meaning of the "time and times and the dividing of time" (Daniel 7:25), "a time, times, and an half" (Daniel 12:7; Revelation 12:14), "forty and two months" (Revelation 11:2), and "a thousand two hundred and threescore days" (Revelation 11:3; 12:6).

During the first half of the "week" (3½ years) the "man of sin" will be occupied with the building of his kingdom. He will arise as a new leader, the little horn among the ten kingdoms (ten horns). He is the rider on the white horse going forth conquering and to conquer (Revelation 6:2). He comes into prominence with the revival of the Roman Empire. All other national leaders will reign with him, but will be under his rule. At the end of the first three and one-half years he will have gained world supremacy, having received his power and authority from the devil (Revelation 13:2).

Kenneth A. Wuest has said,

> Another thing that will characterize the first 3½ years of Daniel's seventieth week is the religious toleration which Antichrist will accord the subject peoples under his sway. The policy of the Roman Empire of the first century was that of religious toleration

granted its subject peoples under two conditions, first that their religions do not come into conflict with the state religion, Emperor worship, and second, that the populace add to its own list of gods the Emperor as a divinity to be worshipped. Christianity came into conflict with Rome on the two scores, proclaiming a God beside whom there is no other, and refusing to worship the Emperor. But Antichrist as Emperor of the Revived Roman empire will temporarily break precedent with first century Rome in that he will grant religious toleration without setting himself up as a god to be worshipped, but will change his policy of religious toleration at the end of the first half of the seven year period, destroy all religious worship and institute Emperor worship as the state religion of the Empire.

During this time of religious toleration, the Jewish remnant of 144,000 Jews, sovereignly chosen to salvation for a special ministry during this 3½ year period (Revelation 7:1-8), will preach the gospel of the kingdom (Matthew 24:14) to the end of the earth. This gospel is the same message which John the Baptist and the Messiah preached (Matthew 3:1, 2; 9:35), announcing the Messiah to establish the earthly kingdom of Israel and offering salvation from sin through this same Messiah. In the time of Antichrist the message will announce the second Advent of Messiah to become earth ruler over Israel and the Gentile nations and offer salvation through His precious blood. Antichrist can do nothing about it, for he as a benevolent dictator will grant religious toleration to Israel. As a result, Gentiles and Jews from every nation (John says, "a great multitude which no man could number of all nations, and kindreds, and peoples, and tongues") will accept the message and be saved (Revelation 7:9-17).

The real purpose of the Tribulation will be accomplished during the last three and one-half years. The Tribulation does not deal at all with the Church, but with Israel. The whole emphasis of the Tribulation is primarily Jewish. Any season of peace and prosperity after the rapture of the Church, and during the first half of the seven years, is a clever ruse on the part of the "man of sin" to gain the confidence of the Jew. In the midst of the "week" he will turn against the Jews and make the Temple desolate with his abominations (Daniel 9:27). Then will commence an outpouring of divine judgment unprecedented in world history.

The Tribulation that is to come will be from God, an outpouring of His wrath. It is divinely planned and it has a divine purpose. It was an important subject of Old Testament prophecy: "When thou art in tribulation, and all these things are come upon thee, even in the latter days, if thou turn to the LORD thy God, and shalt be obedient unto His voice; (For the LORD thy God is a merciful God;) he will not forsake thee, neither destroy thee, nor forget the covenant of thy fathers which he sware unto them" (Deuteronomy 4:30, 31).

"For thus saith the LORD; We have heard a voice of trembling, of fear, and not of peace. Ask ye now, and see whether a man doth travail with child? wherefore do I see every man with his hands on his loins, as a woman in travail, and all faces are turned into paleness? Alas! for that day is great, so that none is like it: it is even the time of Jacob's trouble; but he shall be saved out of it" (Jeremiah 30:5-7).

"And at that time shall Michael stand up, the great prince which standeth for the children of thy people: and there shall be a time of trouble, such as never was since there was a nation even to that same time: and at that time thy people shall be delivered, every one that shall be found written in the book" (Daniel 12:1).

"And it shall come to pass, that in all the land, saith the LORD, two parts therein shall be cut off and die; but the third shall be left therein. And I will bring the third part through the fire, and will refine them as silver is refined, and will try them as gold is tried: they shall call on my name, and I will hear them: I will say, It is my people: and they shall say, The LORD is my God" (Zechariah 13:8, 9).

From these passages we may conclude that in the short space of three and one-half years there will be misery and unprecedented fury sent by God, the "man of sin" being the instrument in its administration. It will be divine judgment, God's dealings with His ancient people prior to the fulfillment of the promised kingdom. If any one questions that God will use the "man of sin" to punish His people, let him recall the many instances in the Old Testament when He used pagan nations to scourge Israel. Truly He makes the wrath of men to praise Him. While the Tribulation will be a time of bringing judgment upon the nations (Isaiah 13:11; 24:21; 26:21; Jeremiah 30:11), it will be primarily the time of "Jacob's trouble." God will accomplish these judgments before the millennial reign of Christ, therefore they must be finished by the end of the seventieth week. "And except those days should be shortened, there should no flesh

be saved: but for the elect's sake those days shall be shortened"
(Matthew 24:22). God in His mercy will not permit a longer
duration.

The Doom of the Man of Sin

When the purposes of God in judgment have been accomplished,
He will then direct His activities in judgment against the "man of
sin." There is no doubt that the entire earth will feel the impact
of these judgments, however the territory of the revived Roman
Empire will be the focal point. The dwellers of earth have defied
God and denied His Anointed, and now they must be made to
repent of their evil (Revelation 9:20, 21).

An excellent condensed description of this last great judgment in
the earth is given to us by Dr. Unger in his most enlightening book,
Biblical Demonology. He says,

> The destroyer of Satan's evil world system will be the all-glorious
> returning Christ, He who at the cross "spoiled principalities and
> powers," and "made a show of them openly, triumphing over them
> in it" (Colossians 2:15), and who thereby not only purchased man's
> redemption, but at the same time redeemed the earth from Satan's
> ultimate usurpation. He who alone was found worthy to unloose the
> seven-sealed book, the title deed to the earth, by virtue of His sacri-
> fice (Revelation 5:1-7), will then have finished opening the seals
> and loosing the judgments upon the earth that will result in the utter
> annihilation of the Satanic system and the dispossession of Satan.
>
> At the end of the Great Tribulation the confederated armies
> under the Antichrist, Satan's tool, will be assembled in the plain of
> Megiddo, in preparation for moving against Jerusalem (Zechariah
> 14:2) to annihilate the Jew. Pouring the "spirit of grace and sup-
> plications upon the house of David" (Israel) and the inhabitant of
> Jerusalem (Zechariah 12:10), the glorious Christ, leading the
> "armies of heaven," will come to their rescue (Revelation 19:11-16),
> clashing with the Antichrist and the wicked kings and their de-
> monized armies of earth, assembled by unparalleled demon ac-
> tivity (Revelation 16:13-16) to make war against the Lord. The
> Beast (Antichrist) and the False Prophet, his helper, will be
> taken and "cast alive into the lake of fire," and their armies "slain
> with the sword of him that sat upon the horse" (Revelation 19:20,
> 21). In the terrific carnage "all the fowls will be filled with their
> flesh" (Revelation 19:21).
>
> The last event marking the collapse of the Satanic world system
> will be the descent of an angel from heaven, who seizes "the dragon,
> that old serpent, which is the Devil, and Satan, and bound (will

bind) him a thousand years," and "cast him into the bottomless pit and shut him up, and set a seal upon him, that he should deceive the nations no more, till the thousand years should be fulfilled" (Revelation 20:1-3). Although only Satan, as the great head of the kingdom of darkness, is mentioned as incarcerated in the bottomless pit, it would be inconceivable in view of the nature of the Messianic Kingdom to suppose that the demon powers were left free to act. In this case the whole body of spiritual evil is to be thought of as included in the head, especially as the bottomless pit is also the prison house of the demons (cf. Revelation 9:1-11).

With the satanic system destroyed and Satan and demons locked up, the time will have at last come for the restoration of the kingdom to Israel (Acts 1:6), that glorious era of peace and blessing so magnificently predicted by the seers of the Old Testament.

There is nothing in all literature so filled with awe as the inspired predictions of that coming judgment. "Behold, the day of the LORD cometh, and thy spoil shall be divided in the midst of thee. For I will gather all nations against Jerusalem to battle; and the city shall be taken, and the houses rifled, and the women ravished; and half of the city shall go forth into captivity, and the residue of the people shall not be cut off from the city. Then shall the LORD go forth, and fight against those nations, as when he fought in the day of battle" (Zechariah 14:1-3).

Another prophet adds a further inspired word to this scene of coming doom. "For, behold, in those days, and in that time, when I shall bring again the captivity of Judah and Jerusalem, I will also gather all nations, and will bring them down into the valley of Jehoshaphat, and will plead with them there for my people and for my heritage Israel, whom they have scattered among the nations, and parted my land" (Joel 3:1, 2).

This is not the final judgment. At the end of the thousand years the remaining dead shall be raised to stand before the Great White Throne, where men who have refused the grace of God in Christ will be judged (Revelation 20:11-15).

This dark and gloomy judgment, yet future, shall not befall the children of God. Because Christ bore the believing sinner's judgment at Calvary, there is therefore no condemnation awaiting him (Romans 8:1). In conclusion we must implore any unsaved person into whose hands this book may come, to receive Jesus Christ as Saviour and Lord at once, and He will give you eternal life.

CHAPTER 3

The Coming Doom of Russia

Thousands of people now living in the world remember when Russia was an undeveloped nation kept from expanding by Great Britain and other nations. The phenomenal developments within Russia herself, and the expansion of her territorial borders, are well-nigh unbelievable. Add to this the fact that, during the same period of time, Russia has undergone a complete change religiously, from the Greek Orthodox Church, as the recognized state religion, to a communistic, atheistic government with its materialistic ideology, and one is forced to look upon the whole movement as being unprecedented in world history.

Actually her new history-making role is of short duration. At the close of World War I Russia was divided by internal revolutions, so that the present strong-arm, authoritative government is not more than about fifty years old. Here, then, is a nation that, in a little more than the lifetime of one generation, has risen from a near nonentity to a position where she is reaching out for world conquest. It is almost a miracle that so many people have been prepared morally, economically, industrially and ideologically in so short a time. But these are the facts. This extraordinary monstrosity is real, and we must face the matter realistically. Russian power and influence is being felt in every country on the earth, and her communistic philosophy is infiltrating all peoples, even among the uncivilized. A dominant fact for consideration is that Russia threatens to rule the world.

The purposes and policies of Russia pose a deadly threat to the collective security of the free world. In a little more than a generation Russia has brought under her control more people than the Christian Church has contacted with the Gospel of Christ. The Christian Church has not succeeded in stemming the tide of communistic aggression. As an example, "the most Christian Indian State elected a Communist government by free election" (F. G. Schwarz, April, 1959). The Roman Catholic Church has failed to arrest the flow of communistic aggression. Italy, the home of Roman Catholicism, has a larger percentage of Communists in its population than any country in the world, and Communism has gained strength with each succeeding election.

A Major World Problem

The success of communistic aggression thus far in the free world, and the communistic threat to complete the conquest of China and to gain control of the free nations from Burma to Japan, is a major problem confronting all the free peoples in the world. How to oppose this deadly threat has been the major task of the diplomats and statesmen in recent years. Some of these national leaders in the free world are scared, and there is reason for them to be. It has been estimated that there are now more than one billion people under communist control. While it is true that many of them are not Communists, nevertheless, the younger generation among them is being taught and thoroughly trained in the doctrines of Communism in communist-organized and communist-controlled schools.

In an article by David V. Benson, President of "Russia for Christ, Incorporated," and published in *Christianity Today* (April 13, 1959), there appeared the following:

> Recently opened in Ashkabad, the capital of Turkmenistan, near the U.S.S.R. Iranian border, is a *University of Atheism* now offering

a six-month course to further the spread of scientific-atheistic knowledge. Graduates are expected to continue "the struggle against religion."

Little wonder the subject of Communism occupies the minds of more people today possibly than any other subject.

While Communism is a problem world-wide in its proportions, America is concerned about her own future and Communism's relationship to our great democracy. Must we face a bloody purge like that of other countries? Will the rights of the individual be taken from us? Will the American women be ravaged by the communist hordes? Will our young men be driven like animals in labor camps? Will our children and grandchildren be taken from their parents and placed in communist-controlled schools? Certainly no alert person who thinks for himself should be criticized for inquiring about the future of Communism in America.

Communism Dethrones God

I have no "inside" information on Communism. I can relate only what I have read in books, periodicals and newspapers, and that which I have heard while listening to discussions and debates by others. First, let me make the point here that is stated clearly by Dr. John Walvoord in his volume, *The Return of the Lord.*

> Communism is more than a form of government; it is more than mere propaganda on the part of Russia; it is more than just a philosophy of the "have nots" trying to get the possessions of those who "have." As we study Communism in the world today, we find it is more than a mere economic theory.

What, then, is Communism? The basic premise of Communism is its false atheistic doctrine that there is no God. Its program is a satanically inspired, irreligious one, fighting for the control of the human race. From its very inception it has systematically attempted to drive from the minds and hearts of all of its subjects all faith in God. Communism is an all-out war against God.

Mikhail Bakunin (1814-1876), a Russian anarchist, enunciated in his *God and the State,* that which he called his "New Gospel." He wrote,

> Brethren, I come to announce unto you a new gospel, which must penetrate to the very ends of the world. . . . The old world must be destroyed and replaced by a new one. . . . The lie must be stamped out and give way to the Truth. . . . The first lie is God; the second

lie is Right, . . . and when you have freed your minds from the fear of God, and from the childish respect for the fiction of Right, then all the remaining chains that bind you, and which are called science, civilization, property, marriage, morality, and justice, will snap asunder like threads *(Russian Events in the Light of Bible Prophecy,* by Louis S. Bauman).

The Encyclopaedia Brittanica says that "His philosophy struck deep roots only in countries such as Italy, Spain and Russia which were industrially backward and had a large oppressed peasant population" (Volume 2, page 948, 1956 edition). Little wonder that these three countries have in them today a higher percentage of Communists in its population than the other countries of the world.

The adherents to Bakunin's philosophy lost no time in taking advantage of the weakened condition of Russia caused by World War I. In January, 1918, Russia made her first official move to declare war on God. The Soviet of Commissars issued a decree (Article 12), which said, "No church or religious association shall enjoy the rights of judicial persons." There is no record of this edict having ever been rescinded, and we do know that it has been enforced, in spite of the lies by Russian authorities that there is religious liberty. "Freedom of religious worship was rigidily restricted by law to customary gatherings for purely formal worship at some registered meeting place. No Sunday school nor other school or class for the instruction of children in things spiritual was tolerated. On one-sixth of the surface of the earth it became a criminal offense for a mother to teach her child so much as a verse of Scripture" (L. S. Bauman).

Decrees similar to this are enjoined by force upon any country that Russia conquers. When Russia stole Poland, ravaging the land and the people, the "Anti-God Council of Moscow" issued a special decree which said,

> All churches, synagogues, and other religious meeting places are to be closed; the anti-God movement will start founding branches at once in territories occupied by the Red Army; all clergy are suspended; people condemned by the State on account of blasphemy are to be released at once; all laws against anti-God propaganda to be rescinded; an atheistic paper is to be issued by the Anti-God Council in the Polish language; 2,800,000 rubles are to be set apart for organizing the anti-God movement in Poland, and the Russian Ambassador is to initiate it at once.

Were Russia to conquer America, we would receive the same treatment here as has every other nation now occupied by Communism. Think of living in a godless society ruled by godless men. Such a society is a totalitarian state where the inalienable rights, given by God, are deprived the members of that society.

Countess Alexandria Tolstoy was incarcerated in a Russian prison amidst horrible filth and disease. After a lengthy imprisonment she escaped and found refuge in San Francisco, California. After observing life in America she concluded that there were conditions here reminiscent of Russia before the Bolshevik revolution. She said,

> Coming events cast their shadows before in the affairs of the nations, and in America the shadows of revolution are dimly seen and sensed. Your churches are empty. Your young people are following materialistic ideals. The mood of America reminds me of pre-revolutionary Russia. I fear the future of this country. Everywhere, even in theaters and publications, immorality is so commonplace.

Atheism breeds immorality, and immorality must ultimately destroy any nation. And America needs to be awakened to the fact that the religion of Communism is not confined to communist countries. It is slowly creeping in upon us, and in some areas it seems to have a stranglehold. The atheistic philosophy that is behind Russia and Communism is the real enemy of the world and the threatening danger of our day in America. Practical atheism is seen on every hand in the spiritual indifference, the crass materialism, and the social immorality throughout America. Exclude the minority of God-fearing men and women, and it can be said that America is a nation of practical atheists who live as though there were no God in existence. I doubt that one in ten thousand persons begins each day, and goes through it, living as if there were a place called heaven, a place called hell, and a judgment to come when God will reckon with sin and sinners. Countess Tolstoy's statement is worth some serious thought. It might well be that the present way of life in America is Satan's softening up process for the final blow of Communism.

A parable of our Lord warns of the possibility of the communist philosophy of materialism fastening itself upon a man. I am giving the account in full for our serious thought.

> And he said unto them, Take heed, and beware of covetousness: for a man's life consisteth not in the abundance of the things which

he possesseth. And he spake a parable unto them, saying, The ground of a certain rich man brought forth plentifully: And he thought within himself, saying, What shall I do, because I have no room where to bestow my fruits? And he said, This will I do: I will pull down my barns, and build greater; and there will I bestow all my fruits and my goods. And I will say to my soul, Soul, thou hast much goods laid up for many years; take thine ease, eat, drink, and be merry. But God said unto him, Thou fool, this night thy soul shall be required of thee: then whose shall those things be, which thou hast provided? So is he that layeth up treasure for himself, and is not rich toward God (Luke 12:15-21).

The man in the parable was a materialist with a covetous spirit. He was not a capitalist but was a materialistic Communist. We are wrong in assuming that Communists are only those in poverty. Many Communists are wealthy men and women who control substantial investments in property and money. Karl Marx, in his *Communist Manifesto*, insisted that economic forces play the largest part in determining the course of history. He taught that the only real things in the world are material things, and that, for Communists, a spirit world does not exist. This idea is sometimes called "economic determinism," or "the economic determination of history." No one can deny that economic forces do influence the making and molding of history, but to say that they determine solely, or even largely, the course of history, cannot be established.

It is this communistic, materialistic spirit that characterized the certain man in Christ's parable and which is so prevalent among us today. The parable was prompted by a man who said to Christ, "Master, speak to my brother, that he divide the inheritance with me" (Luke 12:13). G. Campbell Morgan has the man saying, "I want some of the *things;* my brother has got all the *things;* tell him to give me some *things.*" And then Morgan adds, "The life of the world today, apart from godliness, is always conditioned by things! Men are relating their lives to things, instead of God." Things! Things! Things! But Jesus said, "a man's life consisteth not in the abundance of the *things* which he possesseth" (verse 15). Then after He gave the parable of the rich "fool" He added, "Then whose shall those *things* be" (verse 20).

God calls Communism foolish and the Communist a fool.

The fool hath said in his heart, There is no God (Psalm 14:1).

The Russian Communist will blatantly deny God with his tongue; the American, church-going Communist, while refusing to declare himself such, says so in his heart and proves he is a Communist by his materialistic way of life. A man may sit in church under the sound of God's things that are of eternal value, while he plans and schemes of his own things that are temporal. It is this materialistic spirit that makes the Communist restless and stirs him to covetousness, aggression, war, murder, plunder and robbery. Christ said it is folly for a man to absorb himself in materialism and life as though there were no God. It is folly for a man to live for worldly goods as though he can enjoy them forever. And yet millions are doing it this very hour. The world looks upon such a man as clever and wise; but God calls him a fool. Indeed, the blind are leading the blind, and unless the heart is turned to God, both will end in hell. "So is he that layeth up treasure for himself, and is not rich toward God" (Luke 12:21).

Bishop Ryle of Liverpool wrote,

> When can it be said of a man that he is rich toward God? Never till he is rich in grace, and rich in faith, and rich in good works! Never till he has applied to Jesus Christ, and bought of him gold tried in the fire (Revelation 3:18)! Never till he has a house not made with hands, eternal in the heavens (2 Corinthians 5:1). Never till he has a name inscribed in the book of life, and is an heir of God and a joint heir with Jesus Christ (Romans 8:17, Galatians 4:7)! Such a man is truly rich. His treasure is incorruptible. His bank never fails. His inheritance fadeth not away (1 Peter 1:4). Man cannot deprive him of it. Death cannot snatch it out of his hands. Riches like these are within reach of every sinner who will come to Christ and receive them.

There is nothing in our Lord's parable that prohibits a man from making wise and proper provision for the future. But the materialist in the parable was a typical Communist, wanting "all" for himself and sharing nothing with others (verse 18). Communism grasps all for itself and gives nothing. This is the spirit Christ condemns. If you say that this parable does not condemn such a life, then what does it condemn? Poverty may have some disadvantages, but riches and the desire for them have wrecked more marriages, broken more homes and damned more souls than poverty ever has.

For the love of money is the root of all evil: which while some coveted after, they have erred from the faith, and pierced themselves through with many sorrows (I Timothy 6:10).

I know that some of you are surprised now that you have read these lines. Possibly you were of the opinion that Communism means to share and share alike. No, never! Under Communism a few men rule an entire country. If the United States were overthrown by a communist country, perhaps fifteen or twenty men would rule our country. All industry would be nationalized. All farms would be taken away from their owners. All business enterprises, small and large, would be seized. Insurance companies would be dissolved, so that no American could receive income from any source whatever. This action would be immediate, drastic, and without appeal. Then the country clubs, swimming pools, and other luxuries would be used for the benefit of the "workers." Now these "workers" are not the masses who labor in the factories, mines and on farms. They are the Party bosses who work for the Party. Actually they are working for themselves. They subjugate the people, making slaves of them, while they live in luxury. To the Communist, total communization means state ownership.

William Z. Foster, long-time head of the communist movement in America, has told us what a communist America would be like. Here are his own words:

> Under the dictatorship all the capitalist parties—Republican, Democratic, Progressive, Socialist, etc. — will be liquidated, the Communist Party functioning alone as the Party of the toiling masses. Likewise, will be dissolved all other organizations that are political props of the bourgeois rule, including Chambers of Commerce, employers' associations, Rotary clubs, American Legion, Y.M.C.A. and such fraternal orders as the Masons, Odd Fellows, Elks, Knights of Columbus, etc.

The masses, while called Communists, are not actually Communists. They have been conquered and subdued by Communists. They are the slaves of the Party bosses and the bosses exploit the masses in order to satisfy their own lust for power and possession.

Communism Deifies Man

If the most serious defect in Communism is its denial of God, a close second is its deifying of man. Marx wrote, "The criticism of religion ends in the doctrine that man is the supreme being for man." When man repudiates God, he is left to fashion a god of his own thinking. Communism's premise that man is divine, and that he needs no other god than himself, is the height of conceit and self-righteousness. It is this doctrine in Marxism that gave rise to Communism's bitter hatred against Jesus Christ. Christ's claim to deity, and the Christian's faith in His deity, have occasioned blasphemous attacks against the Son of God. As recent as 1949 it was reported that Russian communist children were taught to sing the following profane and impious hymn,

> The whole world at last is beginning to see
>   The blight of the world is Jesus.
> Keep out the blight or blighted you'll be;
>   Blighted for life by credulity.
> Once I believed but now I can see
>   The blight of the world is Jesus.

A young Russian, who escaped from an exile camp in the icy desert of Siberia, told of attending a Lenin memorial meeting in Moscow and hearing a high ranking communist commissar tell the following story. During the early stages of the communist civil war, Lenin was interviewed by a foreign newspaperman, who asked him, "What will be your next move after you and the Communist Party have established the Bolshevik dictatorship in Russia?" After a moment of thought, Lenin answered, "We are waging a war for Communism and will continue to fight, even to the last drop of our blood, until we have conquered the entire world." Then pointing to a map of the world, Lenin continued, "Do you see this old world? We are going to destroy and wreck it, and upon the ruins and wreckage we will build a new world in which the Communists *shall be the God,* and if any power, king or God, shall interfere with our plans, we shall destroy that power or king, and smite that God." Give attention to the words, *"The Communists shall be the God."* There you have the philosophy of Communism, the deification of man. The very goal of Communism, namely, a perfect society, without God, is an expression of the sinful pride of man.

The final apostasy at the end of the age is the blasphemous boast that man is God. Antichrist, who is a mere man, sets himself up as the object of worship. The Apostle Paul describes it as follows:

> Let no man deceive you by any means: for that day shall not come, except there come a falling away first, and that man of sin be revealed, the son of perdition; Who opposeth and exalteth himself

above all that is called God, or that is worshipped; so that he as God sitteth in the temple of God, shewing himself that he is God (II Thessalonians 2:3, 4).

Antichrist's religious system denies there is a God, and boasts that man is himself his own God. This detestable doctrine of the divinity of man, faith in oneself, the deifying of the human spirit, is the religion of Communism.

The final movement of apostasy, namely, the self-exaltation of a man who actually declares that he is God, is the goal of Communism. It has its roots in lawlessness. The phrase, "the man of sin" can be read, "the man of lawlessness." The words "sin" and "lawlessness" are interchangeable terms (I John 3:4). Surely there has not been a more lawless nation in the world than Russia. Lawlessness has characterized her actions, since the revolution, more than forty years ago. The Russian communist leaders have had regard for no law. No nation's leaders have walked out of United Nations' sessions, in defiance of national and international law, as have the Russian delegates. They have proved themselves to be masters of lawlessness. They believe they are a law unto themselves. Paul describes the lawless one as he *"who opposeth,"* meaning he who sets himself over against. Atheistic Communism teaches its followers to oppose God and to set themselves against all nations and people who do not think as they think.

The Antichrist is described further as one who *"exalteth himself above all that is called God, or that is worshipped."* He is against all that is said to be divine, that is, against the very concept of deity. Having regard for no power higher than himself, he *"exalteth himself."* The principle of lawlessness, so characteristic in Communism, will finally become embodied in "the man of lawlessness." The "mystery of lawlessness" is already at work. Even now there are many antichrists (II Thessalonians 2:7; I John 2:18). Therefore, we are not to think it strange that one will arise in the end time who will command the worship of men. It happened before in history (Daniel 3), and it is to occur again (Daniel 11:36 cf. Revelation 13). We can see forerunners of the Antichrist in the reckless audacity and ferocious insolence of some Red leaders. The spirit of Communism is the spirit of antichrist. And when he comes in his own name, the impersonation of self-sufficiency and independence, he

will suit the spirit of the age. The hearts of the masses will be ripe
for him and will receive him gladly.

In contrast to the "man of lawlessness," who will be welcomed
by the nations, another Man appeared whom they rejected. He was
"a man of sorrows" (Isaiah 53:3). This Man was meek and lowly,
and He humbly became obedient unto death. He said that He
came to do the will of Him that sent Him. Such humility and
devotedness to God was despicable in their eyes since it only condemned their proud, atheistic hearts. It was the lie of Satan that
distorted their thinking.

And now, with the passing of time, this same spirit of antichrist is
gaining momentum in the world. Communism is satanic in its
reasoning, boasting with its founder,

> . . . I will ascend into heaven, I will exalt my throne above the
> stars of God: I will sit also upon the mount of the congregation,
> in the sides of the north: I will ascend above the heights of the
> clouds; I will be like the most High (Isaiah 14:13, 14).

These blasphemous words are the boast of Lucifer who, because of
his rebellion, was expelled from his lofty position by God. He became the devil, and ever since his expulsion he has dragged millions
down with him by his clever deception that man is his own god.

The Prophetic Outlook for Communism

Communism is basically a religion, not confined to Russia. If
Russia were to be overthrown, Communism would continue to
flourish. True, Russia has spearheaded the movement which has
spread Communism's godless philosophy around the world, but
there is clear teaching in the Bible that this form of godlessness
will continue right on through till the end of the age. If this is a
shock to you, as it was to me when I first realized it, I can only
urge you to take your Bible and examine those Scriptures which
treat of the subject.

We have already examined II Thessalonians 2, and we have seen
that the final apostasy at the end of the age is characterized by the
blasphemous boast that man is God. The religious character of
Communism today has an amazing similarity to the religion of the
Antichrist. This is clearly set forth in Daniel's prophecy. God gave
to Daniel a revelation of a world dictator, the head of the revived

Roman Empire. He is described as one who exalts himself above his fellow men and above all gods and God.

> He shall exalt himself, and magnify himself above every god, and shall speak marvellous things against the God of gods (Daniel 11:36).

This king is to come in the "latter days" (Daniel 10:14), in "the time of the end" (Daniel 11:35). He is a counterfeit Messiah, the personal Antichrist, so called by the Apostle John (I John 2:18-22; 4:3; II John 7). Our Lord said,

> I am come in my Father's name, and ye receive me not: if another shall come in his own name, him ye will receive (John 5:43).

There is also a description of the religious system of the Antichrist.

> Neither shall he regard the gods of his fathers, nor the desire of women, nor regard any god; for he shall magnify himself above all. But in his place shall he honor the god of fortresses; and a god whom his fathers knew not shall he honor with gold, and silver, and with precious stones and pleasant things (Daniel 11:37, 38, ASV).

Here is a religion that is almost identical to present-day Communism. The official religion of Communism is a denial of the God of the Bible.

We have pointed out how Communism despises, and even caricatures Jesus Christ. The Scripture says that the Antichrist shall not regard *"the Desire of women."* I have capitalized the word "Desire" because I believe there is only One to whom the word refers here. He is the Lord Jesus Christ, "the Desire of all nations" (Haggai 2:7). H. A. Ironside has written,

> Every Jewish woman hoped that it might be the will of God that through her the Messiah would be born into the world. He was emphatically the Desire of women. Antichrist utterly disregards Him, pretending to be himself the predicted One.

When God promised that Christ would be the seed of the woman (Genesis 3:15), Eve's expectation was that she would be His mother. When her first son was born, she said, "I have gotten a man from the LORD" (Genesis 4:1). No doubt there was the hope in Eve's heart that her son would be the promised Seed.

Finally, we are told that the Antichrist shall honor *"the god of forces."* Some versions translate the word "forces" to read "fortresses." Dr. De Haan believed the god of forces is literally the god of nature.

In this atomic age we can readily understand how this Man of Sin will hold up the discoveries of science, especially the release of atomic energy, as the hope of the world which he will dominate at that time.

Dr. Walvoord believes the god of fortresses is military power personified, the only god Communism knows.

Communism worships power, and this future world dictator will worship power also. Such will be the character of his religion.

Communism's religion of atheism, materialism and the supression of all peoples by force, will continue to grow in the earth. This is the real danger that faces the world, and I see no hope for its defeat. After the Church is caught away to be with the Lord, the blasphemy, unbelief, and ruthless tactics of Communism will seize the world. A more vivid description of those days is depicted in Revelation 13.

But what can Christians do in the face of all this? What conclusions may we draw from these facts? What should be our approach? First, we must do all in our power to proclaim the Gospel to the uttermost part of the earth by every means at our disposal. Second, we should study our Bibles and teach the Scriptures to others. Ministers, Sunday school teachers and youth directors should teach the Word of God. Parents should study the Bible and teach it to their children. Those persons who are instructed in the Scriptures will never become Communists. Moreover, they will be sufficiently conversant with God's plan of salvation so that they can witness effectively to others.

Friend, are you promoting the cause of Jesus Christ? Are you praying, witnessing, giving, and helping in whatever way you are able in order that men shall hear the Gospel and be saved? This is our task!

Russia as a Nation

It is essential that we bear in mind the fact that, even though Communism was bred in Russia, it does not need Russia any longer in order to expand. True, Russia has been the driving force behind its progress. But China might serve as an example of a communist regime gaining strength through her own efforts. The Chinese Communists learned fast from the Russians, and they are well-able to operate independently, without aid from Russia. Even now there are rumors of a break of Red China from Red Russia, and such a division would not take the world by surprise.

What is Russia's future as a nation? The prophetic Scriptures are clear that Communism, at least the philosophy of Communism, will gain in influence as the age draws to a close. The Scriptures are equally clear as to Russia's future as a nation.

First of all, the Bible makes it clear as to where we are in a divinely predicted program. Our Lord used a significant term in His prophetic discourses, namely, *"the times of the Gentiles"* (Luke 21:24). Exactly what did He mean by this? There was a time in Israel's history when Jehovah removed His throne from Jerusalem and permitted a Gentile king to rule over the nations, and over the Jews in particular. The Scriptures are clear that this period, which Christ called "the times of the Gentiles," is clearly marked as to its beginning and ending. The times of the Gentiles will run its course, and the Jewish clock will begin again to tick. The Jewish nation will be restored to the land (Jeremiah 23:3, 4), and there will come a world Ruler, a King who shall rule righteously in the earth (Jeremiah 23:5). This world Ruler is David's righteous Branch, Israel's Messiah, the Lord Jesus Christ.

When did this period commence, and when will it end? The first Gentile world-ruler was Nebuchadnezzar, king of Babylon. God first sent him to lead His people, the Jews, away captive. Had the Jews continued in obedience and faithfulness to God, there never would have been an era of Gentile supremacy. God had said to Israel,

> The Lord shall establish thee an holy people unto himself, as he hath sworn unto thee, if thou shalt keep the commandments of the Lord thy God, and walk in his ways. And all people of the earth shall see that thou art called by the name of the Lord; and they shall be afraid of thee . . . The Lord shall bring thee, and thy king which thou shalt set over thee, unto a nation which neither thou nor thy fathers have known; and there shalt thou serve other gods, wood and stone. And thou shalt become an astonishment, a proverb, and a byword, among all nations whither the Lord shall lead thee (Deuteronomy 28:9, 10, 36, 37).

Dr. J. H. McComb points out that it is a rather startling confirmation of this prophecy when we note that the Hebrew word for "byword" is *Sheninah,* which is surprisingly close to "Sheeni," the term of reproach the Jew despises today. Despite these warnings from the Lord, the Jews disobeyed Him, and He sent Nebuchadnezzar as the instrument of judgment. Nebuchadnezzar appeared the first time in 606 B.C. and led away a group of Jews. He appeared again in 598 B.C. and led a second deportation to Babylon including the prophet-priest, Ezekiel. His final invasion came in 587 B.C., which resulted in the complete subjugation of the Jews.

Among the captives in the first invasion were Daniel and his three companions. It was probably of them that Isaiah prophesied,

> . . . Hear the word of the LORD of hosts; Behold the days come, that all that is in thine house, and that which thy fathers have laid up in store until this day, shall be carried to Babylon: nothing shall be left, saith the LORD. And of thy sons that shall issue from thee, which thou shalt beget, shall they take away; and they shall be eunuchs in the palace of the king of Babylon (Isaiah 39:5-7).

The young man Daniel soon rose to prominence and was made Prime Minister of Babylon. This was all in the plan and providence of God, for Daniel was to fill an important role, as God's prophet, in relating the rise and fall of Gentile power in the earth. Fundamental to an understanding of God's prophetic plan are the great prophecies of the Book of Daniel, especially chapters 2 and 7, which contain the pre-written history of "the times of the Gentiles."

The first prophetic outline of the course of this period is given in Daniel 2. Nebuchadnezzar dreamed a dream, and in his dream he saw a great image. Upon awaking from sleep he could not recall the dream. Thereupon he sent for his magicians, astrologers and sorcerers, and demanded of them that they tell him his dream. When they insisted such a task impossible, he ordered their execution. At this point Daniel interceded for them and their execution was stayed (verses 1-18). That night God revealed to Daniel both the dream and its interpretation, and Daniel came before Nebuchadnezzar, giving glory to God but taking none unto himself (verses 19-30).

Daniel told Nebuchadnezzar that in his dream the king had seen a great image whose brightness was excellent and whose form was terrible. The image's head was of fine gold, the breast and arms of silver, the belly and thighs of brass, the legs of iron, and the feet part of iron and part of clay (verses 31-33). This huge metallic man, called by some the "Great Colossus," represents the four outstanding empires to arise in their respective order during "the times of the Gentiles." Those four great monarchies to arise were the Babylonian, Medo-Persian, Graeco-Macedonian, and the Roman.

When Daniel interpreted the king's dream, the first great world power was already at its zenith. Of course it was Babylon, for Daniel said to Nebuchadnezzar, "Thou art this head of gold" (2:38). But he added, "And after thee shall arise another kingdom inferior to thee" (2:39). The record of the downfall of the Babylonian Empire in Daniel 5:25-31, is reported in secular history.

The second great world government was known as the kingdom of the Medes and Persians. Now observe that the second world power was to be inferior to the first. Daniel said as much (2:39), and it is suggested in the metals in the image in Nebuchadnezzar's dream, the breast and arms being of silver (2:32), and silver being inferior to gold. This second kingdom is further identified as that of the Medes and Persians (Daniel 8:20).

The third world kingdom is mentioned first by Daniel when he spoke to Nebuchadnezzar of "another third kingdom of brass, which shall bear rule over all the earth" (2:39). Again the metal decreases in value, brass being inferior to silver. Secular history substantiates the fact that the Grecian Empire, under Alexander the Great and his four succeeding generals, was the third Gentile world monarchy. The Grecian Empire succeeded the Medo-Persian Empire in 330 B.C., and it was ruled by Alexander the Great until 323 B.C., at which time he died. His empire was divided among four of his generals, the four parts disappearing one by one until the last, Egypt, was conquered in 30 B.C.

The Bible says little concerning the first three kingdoms, the reason being that Daniel is emphasizing those things which have to do with "the latter days" (10:14), "even to the time of the end" (11:35; see also 2:28, 45). Consequently, he says much more about the fourth and the final kingdoms, both of which are related to the two Advents of Christ to the earth. The fourth monarchy is the last Gentile world kingdom before Christ returns the second time to establish His Kingdom in the earth. We know from secular history, and from the New Testament, that the fourth great world power was Rome. At the time of the Incarnation of the Son of God we read,

> And it came to pass in those days, that there went out a decree from
> Caesar Augustus, that all the world should be taxed (Luke 2:1).

The Roman Empire is represented in the metallic man by two
legs of iron and the feet and toes of part iron and part clay. When
Christ was born, the Gentile nations were passing through the leg
period of the Roman Empire, the Romans controlling most of the
civilized world of that day. I feel quite certain that in Daniel's
day the tiny republic, occupying but a small part of the Italian
peninsula, was not expected to become the ruler of the world. And
yet, within five hundred years after Daniel prophesied, all the
known world was subject to Rome's iron yoke. This fourth kingdom
is described in Daniel 2:40-43.

The image in Nebuchadnezzar's dream teaches an important
lesson, namely, each of the metals which made up the image is
inferior to the one preceding it. It commenced with the head of
gold, then followed in succession the silver, brass and iron. This is
all quite significant inasmuch as it suggests a deterioration in both
quality and cohesion. At the close of the "times of the Gentiles,"
the iron and clay will not mix. They will not hold together. "They
shall not cleave one to another, even as iron is not mixed with clay"
(2:43). The Gentile nations simply will not hold together. Not
even the United Nations will be united.

The Bible says nothing about a fifth Gentile world power. However, there will be another world ruler, described in Nebuchadnezzar's dream as follows,

> Forasmuch as thou sawest that the stone was cut out of the moun-
> tain without hands, and that it brake in pieces the iron, the brass,
> the clay, the silver, and the gold; the great God hath made known
> to the king what shall come to pass hereafter: and the dream is
> certain, and the interpretation thereof sure (Daniel 2:45).

The Stone cut out of the mountain, which shall smite the image
and break it to pieces, is none other than the Lord Jesus Christ.
When He comes, He will put an end to all Gentile rule in the earth
and establish His kingdom. When He came to earth the first time,
He was "the stone which the builders rejected" (Matthew 21:42;
Mark 12:10; Luke 20:17). Today He is still "a stone of stumbling,
and a rock of offence" to His enemies who, being disobedient,
stumble at His Word (I Peter 2:8). This was all foretold by the
prophet Isaiah (Isaiah 8:14). But one day our blessed Lord, that

Stone that shall fall from heaven, will smite the federated world powers. His kingdom is the kingdom to which Daniel refers when he says,

> And in the days of these kings shall the God of heaven set up a kingdom, which shall never be destroyed: and the kingdom shall not be left to other people, but it shall break in pieces and consume all these kingdoms, and it shall stand for ever (Daniel 2:44).

The fifth world empire will have God Himself reigning over it in the Person of His Son, Jesus Christ.

If we are correct in our conclusions, and most of the students of Scripture have come to these same conclusions, then there is no room for another world empire until Jesus Christ returns to earth to reign. Many have attempted to establish a world rule, but all have failed, including Napoleon, Hitler, Mussolini and rulers in Japan. From the time of Jesus Christ to the present, there has been no other world government than the Roman government which exercised power when Christ was born and died.

From the facts before us, then, we conclude that the Bible does not allow for another world empire apart from those already mentioned. We can find nothing in Scripture to lead us to believe that Russia will be able to gain control of the world. Russia as a military power will not be able to dominate the world. When the disciples asked Christ, "What shall be the sign of thy coming, and the end of the world (age)?" (Matthew 24:3), He answered them, "For nation shall rise against nation, and kingdom against kingdom . . ." (Matthew 24:7). Such a condition makes no room for any one nation ruling the world.

There can be little doubt that "the times of the Gentiles" are nearing their end. If the Scripture is to be trusted, the end of Israel is not yet. Contrariwise, Israel is in the process of being restored. The people will be regenerated (Ezekiel 36:22-32), the Temple will be rebuilt and the sacrifices will be reinstituted (Ezekiel 45:18; 47:13-23; Zechariah 14:16). But Israel's greatest blessing will be the presence of the King of kings, earth's next mighty Ruler.

Russia's Place in Prophecy

With the rise of Russia as one of the mighty powers in the world today, it is only natural that one should wonder what place, if any,

Russia has in the prophetic program. Dr. M. R. De Haan has said, "If we were to choose the three most outstanding signs of the coming of Christ, we would have no difficulty in placing the rise of modern Russia among those first three signs." He places the political restoration of the nation of Israel as the first sign, and the rise of Russia as the second.

Most Bible students who interpret literally chapters 38 and 39 of Ezekiel have concluded that the future military invasion of Palestine by a great army which sweeps down from the North is Russia. Following is a part of the prophecy,

> Therefore, son of man, prophesy and say unto Gog, Thus saith the Lord God; In that day when my people of Israel dwelleth safely, shalt thou not know it? And thou shalt come from thy place out of the north parts, thou, and many people with thee, all of them riding upon horses, a great company, and a mighty army: And thou shalt come up against my people of Israel, as a cloud to cover the land; it shall be in the latter days, and I will bring thee against my land, that the heathen may know me, when I shall be sanctified in thee, O Gog, before their eyes (Ezekiel 38:14-16).

First, observe the time of the fulfillment of this prophecy — "in the latter years" (verse 8), "in the latter days" (verse 16), "in that day when my people of Israel dwelleth safely" (verse 14). One day God chose a man, Abram by name, and promised him that from his loins should arise a great nation. Closely associated with this promise was God's unconditional gift of the "land," which we all know to be the land of Palestine (Genesis 12:1-3). God chose the nation of Israel originally, not because they were better than any other nation, but simply because it pleased Him to set His love upon them that He might use them as a repository for His Word, and a human ancestry through which the Messiah would be born. However, when the Jews departed from His clear commands and wilfully followed after other gods, then God scattered them among the other nations. Now for 2500 years the Jew has had no homeland to call his own. He has been persecuted and pushed about from place to place.

But now God is starting to bring the Jews back. God has a future for the Jew in Palestine. The people must be in their own land and all rule and government on earth will have its capital in Jerusalem under the headship of the King of kings, the Lord Jesus

Christ. Let us see what the prophet Isaiah says about the future of the Jews and Palestine.

> And it shall come to pass in *the last days*, that the mountain of the LORD's house shall be established in the top of the mountains, and shall be exalted above the hills; and all nations shall flow into it. And many people shall go and say, Come ye, and let us go to the mountain of the LORD, to the house of the God of Jacob; and he will teach us of his ways, and we will walk in his paths: for out of Zion shall go forth the law, and the word of the LORD from Jerusalem, And he shall judge among the nations, and shall rebuke many people: and they shall beat their swords into plowshares, and their spears into pruninghooks: nation shall not lift up sword against nation, neither shall they learn war any more (Isaiah 2:2-4).

When the prophet says that "He shall judge among the nations" (verse 4), he can be referring to none but Christ, because all judgment has been committed to Him (John 5:22); and that day will be *"the day of the Lord"* (Isaiah 2:12), not Russia's day.

Ezekiel has a further word to say about the preparation for the next world empire.

> And I will bring you out from the people, and will gather you out of the countries wherein ye are scattered, with a mighty hand, and with a stretched out arm, and with fury poured out (Ezekiel 20:34).

Here we see that Israel is to be brought back under God's fury (or wrath). Hitler was an instrument of wrath with his anti-semitic horrors. And we all know that anti-semitism has continued till our day and in our own country. Who will deny this? The bombings of Jewish synagogues in our own United States of America a few years ago were a disgrace to our nation. But in all of this God is driving the Jews back to Palestine. They might be content in some corner of an adopted country, but this is not God's plan for them, for He said,

> I will bring them again into their land that I gave unto their fathers (Jeremiah 16:15).

One final word from Ezekiel will aid the student of Holy Scriptures to see how God is getting ready now for the establishing of the next great world kingdom, whose seat of authority will be in Palestine.

> Therefore say unto the house of Israel, Thus saith the Lord GOD; I do not this for your sakes, O house of Israel, but for mine holy name's sake, which ye have profaned among the heathen, whither

ye went. And I will sanctify my great name, which was profaned among the heathen, which ye have profaned in the midst of them; and the heathen shall know that I am the Lord, saith the Lord God, when I shall be sanctified in you before their eyes. For I will take you from among the heathen, and gather you out of all countries, and will bring you into your own land . . . And ye shall dwell in the land that I gave to your fathers; and ye shall be my people, and I will be your God. . . . And the desolate land shall be tilled, whereas it lay desolate in the sight of all that passed by. . . . Then the heathen that are left round about you shall know that I the Lord build the ruined places, and plant that that was desolate: I the Lord have spoken it, and I will do it (Ezekiel 36:22-24, 28, 34, 36).

This is God's program, and all prophecy must fit into this framework. And it is fitting perfectly. Palestine is beginning to flourish religiously, industrially, scientifically and educationally. Large modern universities have been built, the once deserted land is now occupied with industrious Jews. Huge citrus groves are producing some of the world's finest fruits for export. The inestimable wealth in the Dead Sea and the vast amount of oil have made Palestine the most coveted spot in the world. There is not a nation that does not know of her wealth, and certainly no nation would refuse an opportunity to share in it. But the title deed to this land is spelled out clearly by God Himself when He said to Abram, "Unto thy seed have I given this land, from the river of Egypt unto the great river, the river Euphrates" (Genesis 15:18). When He first called Abram, He said, "Unto thy seed will I give this land" (Genesis 12:7), but now He says, "I have given it." The land was given unconditionally, for all time.

Russia Invades Palestine

Perhaps some of you have been wondering what my comments on Palestine have to do with the prophetic future of Russia. They have much to do with it. The vast potential in Israel is the prize for which the Russian Bear will one day reach. Israel is remarkably situated by land and sea, in relation to the flow of world commerce. It is a natural passageway for transporting the oil of the Middle East.

When Israel was about to celebrate her tenth anniversary as an independent nation, the *New York Times* stated,

During the last year the value of Israel's agriculture increased ten percent, making the current total nearly 200 percent greater than when Israel became a nation in the spring of 1948. In ten years the Israelis have tripled their planted acreage in a nation, roughly the size of New Jersey, that is more than half desert and rock strewn mountainside.

Russia, in her desire for world conquest, will not by-pass this most important, significant and wealthy country. The Red Army will invade Palestine, and when the Russian hordes reach out for the land now being prepared by God for His World Ruler, who is His Son Jesus Christ, Russia will have marched to her doom.

The Bible contains some amazing predictions regarding a "power of the north" who will descend on Israel. This northern power is called "Gog and Magog," and it is mentioned many times in Scripture. Chapter 38 of the Book of Ezekiel speaks of the people who will participate in this invasion.

> And the word of the LORD came unto me, saying, Son of man, set thy face against Gog, the land of Magog, the chief prince of Meshech and Tubal, and prophesy against him, And say, Thus saith the Lord GOD; Behold, I am against thee, O Gog, the chief prince of Meshech and Tubal: And I will turn thee back and put hooks into thy jaws, and I will bring thee forth, and all thine army, horses and horsemen, all of them clothed with all sorts of armour, even a great company with bucklers and shields, all of them handling swords (Ezekiel 38:1-4).

Commenting on this passage, Dr. Barnhouse wrote in *Eternity,*

> When Ezekiel 38:2 speaks of "the chief prince of Meshech and Tubal," the term *chief prince* translates the Hebrew word *Rosh.* In our day the word *Turkey* refers both to a bird and to a nation; in Ezekiel *Rosh* means both *chief prince* and *Russia.* This verse, then, can be read: "Son of man, set your face toward Gog, of the land of Magog, *Rosh,* Meshech and Tubal. . . ."
>
> Now, what about the Meshech? Here we get help from toponymy, the study of place names. For example, we call the capital of France, Paris; but the French say *Paree;* we call the city of canals, Venice; the French call it *Veneez;* the Italians, *Venezia,* while the Germans call it *Vendiq;* but it is the same city. *Meshech* corresponds to Moscow, while *Tubal* has the same root as *Tobolsk,* the chief city of Siberia now renamed. So we can read Ezekiel 38:2 thus: "Son of man, set your face toward Gog, of the land of Magog, Russia, Moscow and Tobolsk."
>
> But did Ezekiel know about Russia? No, he did not; but God did. In Scripture several people are named who did not exist until

long after the prophecy was pronounced. In 1 Kings 13:2 a prophet cried out, "A son shall be born in the house of David, Josiah by name," 300 years before Josiah was born. And Isaiah prophetically addresses Cyrus, king of Persia, by name 150 years before the days of Cyrus (Isaiah 45). Unwilling to accept the fact of revelation, the apostles of higher criticism assert that Isaiah's prophecy was written 150 years later than it was, since no one could have known the name of the Persian king so far in advance.

Because Russia is against God, "Thus says the Lord God: Behold, I am against you, O Gog, Russia, Moscow and Tobolsk; and I will turn you about, and put hooks into your jaws, and I will bring you forth, and all your army, horses and horsemen, all of them clothed in full armor, a great company, all of them with buckler and shield, wielding swords" (Ezekiel 38:3, 4). The word *armor* is not in the original Hebrew, but was put in by the English translators to make sense, for here God lifted the curtain of the future and showed Ezekiel that great army. If the prophet had seen atom bombs, guided missiles, and all the modern implements of war — how could he have described the vision in the language of his day? Even in our time, men had no word for what they saw when the first atom bomb went off. Newspaper reporters described it as "a mushroom cloud"; but it was neither mushroom nor cloud. Perhaps future historians may be amused by our definition, for they will probably have the correct scientific term for that thing of death that appears in the sky when atoms are split on the earth. Likewise Ezekiel saw this army of the future and recorded it in the vocabulary of his day.

Ezekiel declares further that this army will come from the north upon the land of Palestine at a time described as a period of security for Israel in the land.

Therefore, son of man, prophesy, and say unto Gog, Thus saith the Lord GOD; In that day when my people of Israel dwelleth safely, shalt thou not know it? And thou shalt come from thy place out of the north parts, thou, and many people with thee, all of them riding upon horses, a great company and a mighty army: And thou shalt come up against my people of Israel, as a cloud to cover the land; it shall be in the latter days, and I will bring thee against my land, that the heathen may know me, when I shall be sanctified in thee, O Gog, before their eyes (Ezekiel 38:14-16).

Concerning these verses, Dr. Walvoord writes,

It seems clear according to this word of Scripture that this army will come from the north. If the terms are traced — such as "Rosh" which is close to the word *Russia*, and "Meshech" which many say refers to the city of Moscow — a clear identification can be made in this portion of Scripture of a great army coming down from Russia upon the land of Palestine. This is confirmed by the fact that the army comes from the north.

Furthermore, the time of the invasion is described in two sentences: it is first declared specifically to occur in "the latter days," and then also, it is described as occurring in a time "when . . . Israel dwelleth securely." Israel is not dwelling securely, or at rest, today in any real sense of the word. We all know of the tension which exists in the land of Palestine. Prophecy reveals that, after the church has been taken home to glory the head of the revived Roman Empire is going to enter into a contract with the Jewish people. In that agreement he is going to offer them protection with the result that Israel will return to Palestine in even greater numbers than we have seen in recent days. They will dwell securely, not because they have an army of their own, but because they are under the protection of this Gentile ruler. Apparently, the battle that is pictured in Ezekiel 38 will occur during the first half of that last seven-year period leading up to the second coming of Christ to establish His kingdom in the world, possibly just preceding the beginning of the last three and one-half years, called the "great tribulation."

Russia Marches to Her Doom

What happens to this great army that comes down from the north to attack Palestine is described likewise by Ezekiel,

> Therefore, thou son of man, prophesy against Gog, and say, Thus saith the Lord GOD: Behold, I am against thee, O Gog, the chief prince of Meshech and Tubal: And I will turn thee back, and leave but the sixth part of thee, and will cause thee to come up from the north parts, and will bring thee upon the mountains of Israel: And I will smite thy bow out of thy left hand, and will cause thine arrows to fall out of thy right hand. Thou shalt fall upon the mountains of Israel, thou, and all thy bands, and the people that is with thee: I will give thee unto the ravenous birds of every sort, and to the beasts of the field to be devoured (Ezekiel 39:1-4).

The Russian hordes will be reduced to one-sixth of the original number, her military might will be destroyed, and the remains of her army will be driven back to the wastes of Siberia. Russia as a military power can never gain control of the world, because it is necessary that she take Palestine in order to have world dominion, and this she will never do.

Gog's fight against God, and his determination to rule the world will be exposed one day before all nations. If you are numbered among the many who wonder why the Lord permits atheistic Russia to continue in her cruel, satanic course, and seemingly to prosper in her evil ways, be patient. God will judge her as He has brought to nought every other inflated dictator who persecuted His people and plundered the earth for profit. God says, "I am against thee, O Gog" (Ezekiel 39:1). While it is true that if God be for us, no one can stand against us, it is equally true that if God is against a man or a nation, no power can spare when God strikes in judgment. Maybe I cannot answer fully the cry of some faint-hearted sufferer, under the heel of Russian tyranny, as to why God permits a nation like Russia to continue. God's ways are past tracing out (Romans 11:34), but do not forget that it is written also,

> Surely the wrath of man shall praise thee: the remainder of wrath shalt thou restrain (Psalm 76:10).

When Gog invades Israel, then God will smite with a violence that will repay Russia for every act of aggression, violence, indecency, unfairness, untruth and dishonesty. God says, "To me belongeth vengeance and recompense" (Deuteronomy 32:35; Psalm 94:1; Romans 12:19). When Russia strikes Palestine, God will strike Russia. We must be patient and wait on the Lord.

The Christian's Hope

The rise of Russia is one of the significant signs of the times which points to the return of Christ to take His own out of this world. It is not until after the Church is raptured that the man of sin, the Antichrist, will show himself. It is not until then that the king of the North will strike. There is only one hope for the child of God. It is "that blessed hope" of Christ's return for His Church (Titus 2:13). It seems that man is reaching his last extremity. How comforting for the true believer in the Lord Jesus Christ to know that soon, possibly in the lifetime of this generation, he will be with his Lord and Redeemer!

In the light of these world-shaking events, are you ready for the coming of the Lord? When He comes He will gather His own unto Himself, but to all who reject Him now, it will mean the last opportunity to be saved, and the beginning of eternal doom. Trust Christ at once lest, for you, it will be eternally too late.

CHAPTER 4

The Coming World Conflict

Some subjects in the Bible are not easy to speak or to write about. It is much easier to bear the good news of salvation than to announce the coming of doom and destruction. No doctor delights to tell the sad news of prolonged suffering or coming death, and yet he cannot escape the facts and evidence of a careful diagnosis. In all fairness the physician finds it necessary at times to reveal that the future is a dark one for certain of his patients.

The writer has found much delight expounding the love and grace of God in the salvation offered through faith in the Lord Jesus Christ, for indeed the future is bright with prospect for all who have trusted the Saviour. But there is a dark side to the future, marked with horrible devastation and bloody death. Such awaits the world of unbelieving men and women who have not been born again into the family of God. It will have its consummation in a literal conflict on earth of unprecedented proportions. This mighty conflict is referred to as "Armageddon."

The word "Armageddon" appears once in Scripture. John writes:

81

"And he gathered them together into a place called in the Hebrew tongue *Armageddon*" (Revelation 16:16). The word is sometimes rendered "Har-Megiddo." "Har" means mountains. "Megiddo" means slaughter. The two words together may be translated "The Mount of Slaughter." In the eternal counsels of God there is a place, the Valley of Megiddo, where King Josiah, of the southern kingdom of Judah, was mortally wounded in the battle against Pharaoh-Necho (II Chronicles 35:22-24), and where the most awful conflict of human history will take place.

Human History Is Written in Blood

Records prove that human history is written in the blood of millions who have died on the world's battlefields, with millions more following to their death as the result of war's horrible aftermath. Someone has estimated that well over 600 million (600,-000,000) deaths have occurred on the fields of battle while millions more were left helplessly wounded to suffer disfigurement and to be left hopelessly crippled for life.

Famine, pestilence, and suffering have followed every war. It was reported recently that one-third of the world's population is facing starvation. In some countries the proportion of tuberculosis among children reaches as high as 75 per cent. It is a matter of record that the destruction of the natural resources of the earth and of human life as the result of war has been followed by increased famine, suffering, pestilence and death.

Look into American history and you will find that our nation has averaged a war about every twenty-five years. Begin with the War of Independence in 1776; add to it the War of 1812, the Mexican War of 1845, the Civil War of 1861-65, the Spanish-American War of 1898, World War I of 1914-18, World War II, the Korean conflict and the war in Viet Nam. There you have it! Scarcely a generation has passed in which this so-called Christian nation has not sent its young men into battle. And I am not unpatriotic nor disloyal when I tell you that I see no hope for peace in this land or other lands before the personal return of our Lord Jesus Christ to the earth.

Human Efforts at Peace Have Failed

Many sincere attempts have been made to put an end to wars. Many peace pacts have been made between nations, but all have

been set aside. Many committees and organizations were formed
to establish peace on the earth, only to break up without success.
Now there is something commendable about these men and their
programs which contemplate a world order without a war. Certainly
they suggest to us that there is a craving for something higher
than bloodshedding. But the idealism that dominates the thinking
of such men is purely human rationalism apart from the plain teaching of God's Word. There is something within each of us which
welcomes with enthusiasm the very thoughts of world peace, but
no amount of wishful thinking about abolishing war will ever
bring it to pass. Such optimistic idealism is purely human reasoning,
but we will never be able to rationalize life to eliminate wars among
men. Even though millions pledge themselves to non-violence,
pledges will never bring the desired peace. No one can deny that
it has failed thus far. No one can assure us that it will succeed at
any time. While the United Nations Organization carries on its
money-spending program, nations are ready to spring at one another like savage beasts. Peace treaties and peace conferences are
powerless to restrain in man the lust for power and wealth and the
desire for revenge.

Will There Ever Be an Age of Peace?

No doubt many have been asking if the golden age of peace, for
which the world has been looking for so long, will ever come.
Certainly the inspired writers of the Old Testament encouraged
Israel to expect an era of universal peace. David looked beyond the
strife in the earth to a blissful season of peace when he wrote: "The
LORD will bless His people with peace" (Psalm 29:11), and "The
mountains shall bring peace to the people" (Psalm 72:3).

The mighty prophet Isaiah encouraged the nation when he wrote:
"And all thy children shall be taught of the LORD; and great shall
be the peace of thy children" (54:13). "For ye shall go out with
joy, and be led forth with peace" (55:12). Here God promises un-
speakable blessing for Israel and a time when they will not have
to fight their foes or flee from them.

Through the prophet Jeremiah God spoke again. It was while
Judah was held in captivity by Babylon that God comforted his
people, saying: "For I know the thoughts that I think toward you,
saith the LORD, thoughts of peace, and not of evil, to give you an

expected end" (29:11). If they desire peace, He would have them know that peace was His desire for them also. No doubt this verse applied directly to deliverance from that immediate captivity, but its larger application had to do with Israel's permanent peace in her own land, for the Lord added: "Behold, I will bring it health and cure, and I will cure them, and will reveal unto them the abundance of peace and truth" (33:6). Jerusalem and the Jews are yet to be cured of the attacks of their enemies. What Jerusalem has been unable to do God will do. He will give to His people the long promised peace.

The predictions of the post-exilic prophets are proof sufficient that God had a plan for world peace. Haggai wrote: "The glory of this latter house shall be greater than of the former, saith the LORD of hosts: and in this place will I give peace, saith the LORD of hosts" (2:9). Here it is clear that God was moving on in His plan to a great event involving all nations, for He said: "I will shake all nations, and the desire of all nations shall come" (2:7). All God's methods are progressive, so that the desire of the nations for peace could not be fulfilled until God had dealt with all nations for their sins. Haggai was a prophet of encouragement to the people, hence he assures the people that the future has brighter hopes in store for them than the past had ever known.

Consider the phrase in Haggai 2:7, "the Desire of all nations." Notice I have capitalized the word "Desire." The long-desired peace must come through the long-desired Person, Israel's Messiah, our Lord Jesus Christ. For centuries the inspired prophets encouraged Israel to look forward, not only to an era of *peace,* but to a *Person* whose name was to be "The Prince of Peace" (Isaiah 9:6). It was to be through the reign of the Son of God that men were to dwell in peace. At the nativity of Jesus the angelic host announced: "Glory to God in the highest, and on earth peace, good will toward men" (Luke 2:14). Christ is a Prince who came to bring peace, but men failed to recognize Him and His purpose, so they rejected His message and spurned His grace. They said: "This is the heir; come, let us kill him, and let us seize on his inheritance" (Matthew 21:38). Men refused the Prince of Peace who alone had the one sure plan to secure lasting peace on earth. This explains why there is no peace in the earth today and why wars and rumors of wars have persisted for the past nineteen hundred years. "The way of peace have they not known" (Romans 3:17).

Wars and Rumors of Wars

After we have read of the bitter treatment that God's Son received at the hands of sinful men in their rejection of His peace plan, we are not surprised to hear our Lord say some thirty years after He came: "Think not that I am come to send peace on earth: I came not to send peace, but a sword" (Matthew 10:34). No contradiction exists here in the purposes of God. The foregoing statement of our Lord discloses that God is permitting men to reap the fruit of their own planting. The coming of Christ set men at variance with the purposes of God and one against another. At his Second Coming He will cause peace to flow like a river, but the effect of His first coming is the badge of war. Where unbelief and opposition to the truth prevail, there can be no peace. Let not my readers, Jewish or Gentile, stumble at Christ's words. With the King and His kingdom rejected, the Prince of Peace Himself absent, the sword must reign. Until He returns, the conflict against righteousness will continue. When He was here, our blessed Lord knew men would reject Him, so He said: "Suppose ye that I am come to give peace on the earth? I tell you, Nay, but rather division" (Luke 12:51).

The military sign is but one of the signs of our times. Jesus said: "And ye shall hear of wars and rumours of wars: see that ye be not troubled: for all these things must come to pass, but the end is not yet. For nation shall rise against nation, and kingdom against kingdom: and there shall be famines, and pestilences, and earthquakes, in divers places. All these are the beginning of sorrows" (Matthew 24:6-8). As He envisioned this present age Jesus told that it would be characterized by a succession of wars. Moreover, global wars involving whole nations would bring this age to its climax. World War I and World War II were terrifying conflicts, but the worst is yet to come. In Mark 13:8 Jesus said that a world war with its "troubles" would be to its inhabitants what birth pangs are to an expectant mother. None will deny that with the passing of time, wars have grown in intensity and furor exactly as the Bible has predicted. And if you want to rid yourself of this predictive element in Scripture, you must rid yourself of the very Scriptures.

Where and When the Conflict Began

Strange as it may appear, this struggle began in heaven, but it will end upon the earth. It began with war between God and Satan, and at times it seemed that the honor went to Satan; but it will end with God overcoming Satan. In Ezekiel 28:11-19 we have a vivid description of Satan before his downfall. In Isaiah 14:12-14 the prophet relates the pride and rebellion of Lucifer, the chief among the angels, who started the great conflict. In Revelation 12:7-12 we have the account of how Lucifer became Satan and was expelled from heaven. How long that initial conflict in heaven lasted or how many angels took part in that first skirmish, there is no way of telling. We do know that the devil was cast out into the earth and his angels with him, and that Michael and his unfallen angels overcame him by the Blood of the Lamb, and by the word of their testimony. God had won the first battle.

Seeing that he could not stand against the Almighty, Satan's next target of attack was against Adam and Eve, the human pair whom God had created and placed in the Garden of Eden. In spite of God's clear warning to our first parents, the Serpent in his subtlety persuaded Eve to eat the forbidden fruit, and she in turn enticed her husband to eat. Adam and Eve fell from their lofty estate and lost the divine moral likeness and their immortality. Satan appeared to win the second round.

At this point it is well to notice that God said: "And I will put enmity between thee and the woman, and between thy seed and her seed; it shall bruise thy head, and thou shalt bruise his heel" (Genesis 3:15). If Satan was determined to carry the fight, then God would not suffer the enmity to die down. Keep in mind here that God is not the author of the enmity, that is, He did not arouse Satan to enmity or He would be the author of evil. Satan started the conflict, but God is going to see it through to the triumph of righteousness. This verse reveals a further unfolding of the clash between the Seed of the Serpent and the Seed of the woman, with the Seed of the woman ultimately triumphing over the Seed of Satan. In other words, the battle is to be fought out to a decisive conclusion and won by Jesus Christ. The Seed of the woman (Christ) suffers, but Satan is seen to be crushed. Here on the first pages of the Bible God pronounces the age-long struggle culminating in a mighty triumph of Jesus Christ and the sentence of doom upon Satan. Armageddon will be the decisive battle.

Satan's Attack Continues

All through the past six millenniums of human history there were times when it seemed that Satan would conquer. Adam and Eve had two sons named Cain and Abel. Abel followed in the way of the Lord. Then one day Cain rose up and killed his brother Abel. Again it seemed that victory in the contest would go to Satan, but God preserved the holy Seed by giving Adam and Eve another son, Seth (Genesis 4).

The years went by, the population in the earth increased, and Satan filled the hearts of men with evil. God saw that the wickedness of man was great in the earth, and that every imagination of the thoughts of his heart was only evil continually. It grieved God at His heart until He determined to destroy man from the face of the earth. He sent the great flood to cover the earth, but Satan had so hardened the hearts of the multitudes that they would not turn from their sin. Again it appeared that the forces of evil would win — "But Noah found grace in the eyes of the Lord . . . And God remembered Noah" (Genesis 6:8, 8:1). Again God had preserved the holy Seed.

About 1500 years after the flood "there went a man of the house of Levi, and took to wife a daughter of Levi. And the woman conceived, and bare a son: and when she saw him that he was a goodly child, she hid him three months" (Exodus 2:1, 2). That baby's name was Moses. But why was it necessary to hide the child? The godless Pharaoh, inspired by Satan, conceived a diabolical plot to legalize infanticide as a state policy. The murderous pagan king decreed that every Hebrew son born was to be killed immediately. This was another attempt on Satan's part to frustrate the purposes of God. Every human instrument that God was about to use to keep the godly line intact, until Jesus Christ the royal Seed should come, became the object of Satan's attack. But, glory to God, when Satan begins to show his strength then the Lord begins to act. In divine providence the tiny babe was rescued and reared to become Israel's great leader and law-giver. Again in the face of seeming defeat God preserved the holy Seed.

Less than one hundred years after the death of Solomon, Satan entered the heart of a woman in another attempt to destroy the purpose of God as revealed first in Genesis 3:15. King Ahaziah of the southern kingdom of Judah reigned but one year. The brief rule of this wicked man terminated when he was slain by Jehu. At this point Satan seized the heart of the dead king's mother. "When Athaliah the mother of Ahaziah saw that her son was dead, she arose and destroyed *all the seed royal* of the house of Judah. *But . . .*" (II Chronicles 22:10, 11). Thank God for the Bible "buts." Athaliah only thought she destroyed *all* the seed royal. She destroyed all the seed royal of the house of Judah "but . . . Joash." The daughter of Jehoram hid the boy Joash in a bedchamber where he was cared for during the next six years. Blessed be God for the king's daughters! Again Satan saw that the plan of God was not to be thwarted.

Time marched on. Once again the evil instigator of war rose up in defiance of the Almighty. This time he possessed the heart of Sennacherib, king of Assyria, to lead his armies against the holy city and its godly King Hezekiah of the royal seed of David. Just when it appeared that the holy Seed would be cut off, God intervened and said: "I will defend this city, to save it, for mine own sake, and for my servant David's sake. And it came to pass that night, that the angel of the LORD went out, and smote in the camp of the Assyrians an hundred fourscore and five thousand (185,000): and when they arose early in the morning, behold they were all dead corpses" (II Kings 19:34, 35). Satan was still fighting God, but he was fighting a losing battle.

Eight hundred years went by. The iron rule of Rome held the known world in its power. The throne was occupied by the devil-possessed Herod, a godless Idumean who became Satan's tool in a critical hour of the world's history. In a Bethlehem manger the Seed of the woman was born, the promised One of Genesis 3:15, He who was to crush the head of Satan. Seeing that time was running out Satan fired the heart and mind of Herod with the diabolical scheme similar to that of Pharaoh. He ordered all the children two years old and under to be slain. Mary's young child, God's holy Son, was almost in the enemy's grasp; but all of hell could not stop the plan of God to put an end to war. When he was only thirty-three, Christ's enemies nailed Him to the cross and buried Him in a tomb. But on the third day He arose. Again the Lamb of God, the Lion of the tribe of Judah, had conquered. And ever since Pentecost Satan has been doing his worst to attack the Church of Jesus Christ. For more than sixty centuries a contest between God and Satan has waged.

But time is rapidly running out for Satan and his hordes. He wants to fight, and until Christ returns to crush his head he will continue to wage war. While God has permitted wars to come because of our sins, Satan has been the one responsible for all wars. One last great conflict, however, will end all wars, and this writer believes it is possible that some living on the earth today will be here to suffer and die in that conflict.

Armageddon

This conflict is what we know as Armageddon. As to the *time* of the conflict, it will take place at the close of the Tribulation when Christ returns in person with His saints. All true believers in the Lord Jesus Christ will have been translated at Christ's return for His saints (I Thessalonians 4:16, 17). The preparation for Armageddon is described in Revelation 16:13-16. The consummation of the battle is set forth in Revelation 19:11-21. Armageddon will be the fulfillment of the "smiting stone" of prophecy of Daniel 2:35, 44, 45. The prophecies of Isaiah 10:20-34; 34:1-8; 63:1-4; Zechariah 10:10, 12; 13:8; 14:9; show that the Battle of Armageddon will be by divine appointment. While it is true that the armies of men will be marshaled by Satan, it is by divine appointment nevertheless. The Satan-inspired Beast of the ten-kingdom Western Empire will call his armed forces for the battle. The armies of the United States will be transported to join them. Think of it! Millions of armed men being moved to a given spot for a war that will be made the last war according to divine plan. Study the fulfilled prophecies of Scripture and learn that the plans of God never go amiss.

Consider next the *place* where the battle will be fought. The "Valley of Megiddo" is situated in central Palestine on the edge of the great plains of Esdraelon or Jezreel, and it is named at least twelve times in Scripture. Look at a map and you will see that it lies between the Mediterranean Sea and the Jordan River, a strategic location between Asia Minor and Egypt. That rich valley that has witnessed the rise of many civilizations will one day behold the total overthrow of all Gentile power. Judging by the comments on recent events, there are some eminent observers who believe that a great war is imminent in the East. These men are not all professing Christians nor do they make any claims to belief in the Bible.

As far back as the time of Napoleon, that great leader pronounced it "the most natural battleground of the whole earth." Frederick L. Brooks in his book, *Prophetic Glimpses,* said: "Here many of the most noted military generals have fought. Thothmes fought here 1500 B.C.; Rameses, 1350 B.C.; Sargon, 722 B.C.; Sennacherib, 710 B.C.; Nebuchadnezzar, 606 B.C.; Antiochus Epiphanes, 168 B.C.; Pompey, 63 B.C.; Titus 70 A.D.; Khosru, the Persian King, 614 A.D.; Omar, 637 A.D.; the Crusaders under St. Louis of France, 909 A.D.; Saladin, who conquered Richard the Lionhearted in 1187 A.D.; the Ottoman Forces, 1516 A.D." There Satan and his hordes had met God before. Three renowned mountains overlook this valley: Carmel, Gilboa and Tabor. It was on Mount Carmel where the contest between Elijah's God and the devil-possessed, Baal-worshiping prophets of Jezebel took place. It was one of the mightest conflicts in the Old Testament. It was not a battle of one man versus a nation, but God versus Satan, for on that day "The fire of the LORD fell" (I Kings 18:38). One day it will fall again, but in that day the fire will be accompanied by the Lord Himself, "and his feet shall stand in that day upon the mount of Olives, which is before Jerusalem on the east" (Zechariah 14:4).

Let us look now at the *purpose* of the conflict at Armageddon. I believe Armageddon is the divinely-appointed event through which God will settle once and for all His dealings with the unbelieving Gentile nations of the world who, inspired by the devil and his desire for war, have rejected God's plan of salvation and have allied themselves with the Antichrist to make war against Jerusalem. Armageddon cannot possibly be averted as long as Satan controls the hearts of unregenerated men. The Jew will be in his land at that time and in control of the world's wealth.

In the 1930's we were in the midst of a financial depression, yet the following figures estimate the wealth in the Holy Land at that time. In the deposits of the Dead Sea alone there was reported to be: 1,300,000,000 tons of potash valued at $70,000,000,000; 853,000,000 tons of bromide valued at $260,000,000,000; 11,900,000,- 000 tons of salt valued at $27,500,000,000; 81,000,000 tons of gypsum valued at $120,000,000; 6,000,000,000 tons of calcium chloride valued at $85,000,000,000; 22,000,000,000 tons of magnesium chloride valued at $825,000,000,000, making a total value of $1,267,500,- 000,000, as much, if not more, than all the wealth of the rest of the civilized world. Triple this figure and you have some idea of the worth of these chemicals at today's market prices. Control of the Near East will be the bone of contention. Zionism and the Jewish issue will be the big factors. The contest, in the eyes of the Gentile world powers, is for a prize. Satan will use in that day, as he always has done, wealth and power to trap the unwary. And God, foreseeing that day, has planned to put an end to Satan's rebellion. But the tragedy of it all is the awful judgment that must come to every individual in that day who has not been saved through faith in the Lord Jesus Christ.

The armies of millions of men will be gathered, but before hell breaks loose, heaven intervenes, and a one-sided victory by the Lord Jesus Christ over the hordes of hell will be inevitable. These forces that gather against Jerusalem will come from the whole earth, from among all nations. God said: "I will also gather all nations, and will bring them down into the valley of Jehoshaphat . . ." (Joel 3:2). "For my determination is to gather the nations, that I may assemble the kingdoms, to pour upon them mine indignation, even all my fierce anger: for all the earth shall be devoured with the fire of my jealousy" (Zephaniah 3:8). "I will make Jerusalem a burdensome stone for all people . . . though all the people of the earth be gathered together against it" (Zechariah 12:3). "For I will gather all nations against Jerusalem to battle . . . Then shall the LORD go forth, and fight against those nations, as when he fought in the day of battle" (Zechariah 14:2, 3). The nations will gather, not alone for the wealth of Palestine, but with the evil determination to wipe out God's earthly people. All the nations of the earth will be bitten by the virus of anti-Semitism, and while they will not know it at that time, it is clearly taught in God's Word that they will only be positioning themselves for the stroke of divine wrath and judgment.

It will be the last frantic effort to wipe out Israel, but it will be met by the God of Abraham, Isaac and Jacob.

The Lord Is a Man of War

Many see only one side of the divine nature, namely, God's love and mercy, and overlook His holiness and justice. Throughout the Bible and in human experience, clear consistent teaching on the God-given and unalterable law of sowing and reaping appears (Galatians 6:7). He that soweth to the flesh must reap the corruption that follows. Sin pays wages. When God miraculously slayed the entire Egyptian army in delivering His people from Pharaoh, Moses sang: "The LORD is a man of war (Exodus 15:3). God has waged war on numerous occasions in the past and He will do it again. He will fight again "as when he fought in the day of battle" (Zechariah 14:3). He fought for his people at the Red Sea (Exodus 14:25), at Jericho (Joshua 6:20), at Gibeon (Joshua 10:8-14), at Megiddo (Judges 4:15, 5:20), at Mizpeh (I Samuel 7:10), and at Jerusalem (II Kings 19:35). And at that very site where He smote the Assyrians once, He will do it again.

The Nature of the Conflict

Most naturally the question arises as to how our Lord will wipe out the Gentile armies of the world. Certainly the outcome of the battle will not depend upon the Church, the Bride of Christ who comes with Him, nor upon Israel and its leaders. Vivid prophetic figures depict the awful devastation to be inflicted upon Israel's foes, one of these being fire — "In that day will I make the governors of Judah like an hearth of fire among the wood, and like a torch of fire in a sheaf; and they shall devour all the people round about, on the right hand and on the left: and Jerusalem shall be inhabited again in her own place, even in Jerusalem" (Zechariah 12:6).

The consuming power of fire is quite well-known both to Bible students and to all who have ever had experience with fire. We merely cite here the case of Samson (Judges 15:1-5) and Absalom (II Samuel 14:28-30). There are others. No better symbol could be chosen for the presence of Jehovah than fire. It is immaterial, terrible, consuming. God appeared to Moses in a flame of fire

(Exodus 3:2). He led Israel at night by a pillar of fire (Exodus 13:21, 22), and sent fire mingled with hail to plague the Egyptians (Exodus 9:23, 24). We are told that the Lord descended in fire (Exodus 19:18) and that the glory of the Lord was like devouring fire (Exodus 24:17). Both the Old and New Testaments teach that, "The LORD thy God is a consuming fire" (Deuteronomy 4:24; Hebrews 12:29). There are numerous other passages to be studied about the fire of God, but it will suffice here to say that, as "the fire of God came down from heaven" on previous occasions (see II Kings 1:12), so it will at Armageddon when God settles the controversy with the nations regarding the rejected sovereignty of His Son.

I am not here attempting any discussion on A-bombs or H-bombs. It is enough to say that atomic power belongs to God. When man harnessed the atom into a bomb and dropped the deadly missile on August 6, 1945, textbooks in physics and the whole art of war underwent a thorough revision. Man may have discovered how to harness and use God's atom, but not until Armageddon will the earth know the full strength of fire from heaven. The Apostle Peter gave to us a prophecy concerning a final conflagration on the earth when the elements shall melt with fervent heat (II Peter 3:7-14). Other Biblical references speak of a devouring fire which will descend down from heaven (Psalm 50:3; 97:3; Isaiah 66:15, 16; Ezekiel 20:47, 48; Joel 2:3, 30; Zephaniah 1:18; 3:8; Malachi 4:1).

Concerning Armageddon we conclude with reference to a few passages of Scripture which should cause every unsaved person to pause and consider his need of accepting Jesus Christ. Paul writes: ". . . The Lord Jesus shall be revealed from heaven with his mighty angels, In flaming fire taking vengeance on them that know not God, and that obey not the gospel of our Lord Jesus Christ: Who shall be punished with everlasting destruction from the presence of the Lord, and from the glory of his power" (II Thessalonians 1:7-9). What solemn words! What terrible judgment awaits all who remain after Christ has taken His own out of this world! Divine retribution is inevitable. A solemn infliction of justice must surely come to pass.

John writes: "And the fourth angel poured out his vial upon the sun; and power was given unto him to scorch men with fire. And men were scorched with great heat, and blasphemed the name of

God, which hath power over these plagues: and they repented not to give him glory" (Revelation 16:8, 9). This is Armageddon. How awful will be the torture! How terrible the pain when God settles His quarrel with the nations respecting obedience to the Gospel of His Son! Christ will be victorious and all the redeemed will share His victories.

But to you who have rejected Him, hear the Word of the Lord: "Their flesh shall consume away while they stand upon their feet, and their eyes shall consume away in their holes, and their tongue shall consume away in their mouth" (Zechariah 14:12). The aftermath of the A-Bomb dropped on Hiroshima will have been a light affliction compared with Armageddon.

So devastating will that awful scourge be that the islands of the sea will disappear and the mountain peaks will be leveled because of an earthquake "such as was not since men were upon the earth" (Revelation 16:18-20). This earthquake is foretold in Zechariah 14:4, 5.

The description continues: "And there fell upon men a great hail out of heaven, every stone about the weight of a talent: and men blasphemed God because of the plague of the hail; for the plague thereof was exceeding great" (Revelation 16:21). A professing Christian read that verse and said: "I doubt that." Let there be room in no one's mind for doubt on this or any other descriptive statement concerning the terrible judgments to come upon the earth when Christ returns in glory. Think of it! Even as God plagued the Egyptians with hail (Exodus 9:18-26) and discomfited and slew Israel's enemies in the time of Joshua (Joshua 10:10, 11), even so shall He slay the nations with hail stones weighing as much as 100 pounds when Christ returns to establish His rule in the earth. This will mean conquest over Satan and death and the end of man's rule in the earth.

Then shall there be peace, first in Jerusalem, and then in all the earth. God's plan for the kingdom of the Messiah on earth will be fulfilled. "Then shall the King say unto them on his right hand, Come, ye blessed of my Father, inherit the kingdom prepared for you from the foundation of the world" (Matthew 25:34).

Trust the Saviour now and escape the awful judgment to come.

CHAPTER 5

The Coming Reign of Christ

The greatest Bible expositors of this and past generations are, and were, devout adherents to the doctrine of Christ's return. They believed that Jesus was coming in glory to reign on the earth. The time element of this earthly reign is to be found in the Holy Scriptures. The Apostle John writes,

> Blessed and holy is he that hath part in the first resurrection: on such the second death hath no power, but they shall be priests of God and of Christ, and shall reign with him a thousand years (Revelation 20:6).

The "thousand years" is the term in Scripture which represents that golden age in which our Lord and Saviour Jesus Christ shall return with His saints, visibly and bodily, to establish His kingdom on earth. This "thousand years" is commonly known by the word "millennium," a Latin word compounded of two words: *mille*, a thousand, and *annus*, a year. Though the word "millennium" itself is nowhere found in the Bible, we read six times in Revelation 20 that the kingdom age will last a thousand years.

God's plan, as we see it in His Word, is simply this: our Lord Jesus Christ will come in the air, at which time His Bride, the Church, will be caught up to meet Him (I Thessalonians 4:16, 17).

This is "our gathering together unto him" (II Thessalonians 2:1), known as the Rapture of the saints. It is the comforting hope of all who have been born again. Immediately after the Rapture there will commence that period known as "the Tribulation," seven years of earthly history between the Rapture and the Second Coming of Christ with His saints to reign on the earth. The tribulation period is designated in Scripture by the terms "the great tribulation," "the coming hour of temptation," "the time of Jacob's trouble," "the overspreading of abominations." The Church will not be in the world when the tribulation age is ushered in. Though the Church has known much in the way of trial and tribulation, yet of this specific period of unparalleled tribulation, our Lord has assured her,

> Because thou hast kept the word of my patience, I also will keep thee from the hour of temptation, which shall come upon all the world, to try them that dwell upon the earth (Revelation 3:10).

After the Tribulation, known as Daniel's Seventieth Week (Daniel 9:24-27), Christ will come with His saints to end the Tribulation, and then to execute righteous judgment upon the earth for one thousand years.

Three Millennial Views

One of the main points of difference among teachers has to do with the manner in which the Millennium is to be introduced. Here indeed is the parting of the ways. This is where the three groups, the *premillenarian,* the *postmillenarian,* and the *amillenarian* differ. Let us examine briefly these three views.

A. The *premillenarian* believes that before the millennial age of the kingdom of God can come into the world, our Lord Jesus Christ Himself must return in person. On this teaching we have taken our stand. We believe that, as this age goes on, the Church (the true Church which is Christ's Body) will be less and less influential in the affairs of this world. Instead of the Church overcoming the world, the Church will lose its hold upon the world. War, iniquity and lawlessness will increase, and more and more the civil government of this age will come under the power and influence of Satan. The premillenarian expects that the civil government, as it now exists, must be completely changed or destroyed before the kingdom of God can be established among men. First, however, at some undetermined moment (it could be today), the Lord Himself will appear in the air, raise the dead in Christ, catch up the living believers and take them to be with Him. This translation of the saints means that the Church will escape the Tribulation. After the seventieth week of Daniel, during which time the world is given over to Satanic power, the Lord will descend with his previously-raptured saints to reign for one thousand years. Because we believe that the coming of our Lord must be before the Millennium, we are called premillenarians.

B. The *postmillenarian* believes that the civil and institutional life of man will be gradually transformed through the agency of the Church. He believes that the preaching of the Gospel will have a world-wide influence that will overcome greed, selfishness, hatred and war. He labors to convert men and organizations to think the "Bible-way," thus he believes that the world will grow better and better until, by a gradual change the kingdoms of this world will become the kingdom of God. He believes that the Church will bring in the kingdom, and for a thousand years the ability and genius of man will be displayed. Then, after the Millennium, the Lord will come and separate the goats from the sheep after a general resurrection of the dead.

C. The *amillennial* school teaches that there is not to be an earthly Millennium of any kind at any time, either through a world-wide conversion as a result of the preaching of the Gospel, or through the return of Christ. These teachers hold that God is calling out from the peoples on the earth His Church, and that He will continue to do so until the world comes to an end. They hold that the end of the world will terminate at the return of Christ, at which time there will be one general resurrection and one general judgment, and that Christ will separate the saved from the lost.

Kingdom truth is revealed in both the Old and the New Testaments. Milton would not conclude *Paradise Lost* until he had turned it into *Paradise Regained*. Every age has its men whose aspirations and ambitions were to reach the Paradise that was lost to man. Every man-made effort ended in failure and disappointment, but still there lies within the human breast the hope that man will one day regain the Eden which he lost. While we insist that man's efforts to restore the kingdom of God on earth have failed, still his idea of a kingdom is in perfect harmony with the plan of Almighty God. The literal kingdom of God will be set up on earth, and the time and method of the fulfillment is plainly set forth in the Word of God.

The Church and the Kingdom

Some err greatly in confusing the kingdom with the Church. Well-meaning Christians often fail to distinguish between the two. I have been in churches where pastors, or church officers, have prayed for the advancement of the kingdom. God's purpose for this age is the building of His Church. The kingdom cannot be established until the King returns, and this He will not do until He has finished building His Church. We are living in the Church Age, "the dispensation of the grace of God." This is the "mystery" concerning the Church, a truth not hitherto revealed "which in other ages was not made known unto the sons of men, as it is now revealed unto his holy apostles and prophets by the Spirit." The word "church" in the Greek is "ecclesia," and it means "the called out ones." In this age God is offering a full and free salvation to all men,

> . . . That the Gentiles should be fellowheirs, and of the same body, and partakers of his promise in Christ by the gospel (Ephesians 3:6).

The Church is built gradually, the building program having been in progress now for over nineteen hundred years. In contrast to the gradual building of the Church, the kingdom is set up suddenly when the King returns. The Church is in the present; the kingdom is yet future. The Church Age began after the sufferings and humiliation of Christ on earth, and the Church shares with Him in His humiliation. The kingdom will manifest the glory of Christ. The prophets searched diligently into the Spirit's teaching when He "testified beforehand the sufferings of Christ, and the glory that should follow" (I Peter 1:10, 11).

When we become Christians and members of Christ's Church, we identify ourselves with His sufferings, "crucified with Christ" (Galatians 2:20), "crucified unto the world" (Galatians 6:14).

> Who now rejoice in my sufferings for you, and fill up that which is behind of the afflictions of Christ in my flesh for his body's sake, which is the church (Colossians 1:24).

The Church Age is that of gospel preaching, and suffering and death is involved in taking the Gospel to the uttermost part of the earth. But the kingdom will be a manifestation of His regal splendor and glory when He shall sit in the throne of His glory. Then those who have suffered with Him, and for Him, shall be exalted to authority with Him in that day.

> And Jesus said unto them, Verily I say unto you, That ye which have followed me, in the regeneration when the Son of man shall sit in the throne of his glory, ye also shall sit upon twelve thrones, judging the twelve tribes of Israel (Matthew 19:28).

The Church Age will end at the Rapture, when Jesus comes in the air to catch away the redeemed; the Kingdom Age will not commence until the King returns the second time with His own redeemed ones and all the holy angels with Him.

At no time was the earthly kingdom a mystery. Contrariwise, the coming kingdom on earth was the theme of all the prophets. The history and the future of Israel cannot be rightly understood unless it is viewed from the kingdom standpoint. The Old Testament is replete with vivid descriptions of conditions in the earthly kingdom. Both Jesus and John the Baptist preached, "Repent ye: for the kingdom of heaven is at hand" (Matthew 3:2; 4:17). Then the King was offering Himself to Israel, but Israel rejected her King, and the kingdom was postponed. When Jesus was offering Himself as King, the disciples were preaching "the gospel of the kingdom." But it is not the gospel of the kingdom that the Church is now to preach, but the gospel of the grace of God. The kingdom is not at hand; the Lord is at hand to save all who come unto God by Him. After the Rapture of the Church, Jewish evangelists will once more preach the gospel of the kingdom; then after the Tribulation the King shall return to establish His kingdom. He will not offer Himself to be received or rejected in that day, for He shall rule with a "rod of iron" (Psalm 2:1-3; Revelation 2:26, 27; 12:5). During the present Church Age Christ can be received or rejected by men. We are now living in man's day. But the Kingdom Age will reveal His power and majesty, and He shall rule whether men want Him or not.

The distinguishing characteristic of the Church Age is *grace*. The distinguishing characteristic in the Millennium will be *righteousness.* The grace of God is withholding judgment today, and that is why He permits evil. In the Kingdom Age grace will not prevail, but righteousness shall reign when all the powers of evil are subdued. Failure to distinguish between the Church and the kingdom results in confusion.

Is the Kingdom Spiritual or Literal?

While we are considering here that physical, visible kingdom that has been predicted in many prophecies, we must admit that there is a spiritual kingdom into which all those who believe have entered. But in our agreement with this fact, namely, that all who believe enter into a spiritual kingdom, we take every precautionary measure against spiritualizing the Davidic throne that is to be rebuilt at Jerusalem in the future. In the last analysis the kingdom of God can be defined as that sphere over which God rules, and there is no area in nature, or in human life, over which God does not rule. In one sense of the word the Church is included in the kingdom, simply because God is sovereign over His Church. But the Church is not the kingdom any more than Philadelphia is Pennsylvania. However, just as Philadelphia is in Pennsylvania, and comes under the authority of that State, so the Church is in the kingdom since it is under the authority of the King. The kingdom of God is not interpreted in terms of territory only. The Apostle Paul wrote,

> For the kingdom of God is not meat and drink; but righteousness, and peace, and joy in the Holy Ghost (Romans 14:17).

It is possible to apply this verse to the Pope's decree that Romanists shall not eat meat on certain "holy days." The Romanist idea of ceremonies and abstinence have nothing whatever to do with the kingdom of God. Men do not see the kingdom of God by adhering to any rite or ritual of man, but by being born from above, for,

> . . . Except a man be born again (from above), he cannot see the kingdom of God (John 3:3).

There is a sense in which the kingdom of God is with us in a spiritual way that has nothing whatever to do with days, seasons, ceremonies, food and drink. The moment we were born again we entered into the spiritual sphere of God's kingdom.

This thought can be carried another step so that we can rightly say that the dominion of Satan is in the kingdom. Is not God

Sovereign over all? Certainly Satan is not sovereign over God! Satan and all the fallen angels are subjects, since they operate only by the permissive will of God. Whether the subjects are willing or unwilling subjects, they are limited in their sphere of operations since God is infinitely sovereign. The kingdom of God is all-embracing, wherever there is a subject.

But the above views will not permit a spiritualizing of the Messianic kingdom on earth. Two important passages on the virgin birth of Christ, one in the Old Testament and one in the New Testament, teach clearly, in addition to the virgin birth, the literal reign of Christ upon the throne of David. In Isaiah 9:6, 7, we read,

> For unto us a child is born, unto us a son is given: and the government shall be upon his shoulder: and his name shall be called Wonderful, Counsellor, The mighty God, The everlasting Father, The Prince of Peace. Of the increase of his government and peace there shall be no end, upon the throne of David, and upon his kingdom, to order it, and to establish it with judgment and with justice from henceforth even for ever. The zeal of the LORD of hosts will perform this.

In the classic prophetic utterance on the virgin birth in the New Testament, we read,

> And, behold, thou shalt conceive in thy womb, and bring forth a son, and shalt call his name JESUS. He shall be great, and shall be called the Son of the Highest: and the Lord God shall give unto him the throne of his father David: And he shall reign over the house of Jacob for ever; and of his kingdom there shall be no end (Luke 1:31-33).

We can see, at once, that this twofold revelation of Jesus Christ marks the beginning and ending of His earthly career. The modernist spiritualizes the truths in both of these verses. He insists that neither the virgin birth nor the Davidic throne are to be interpreted literally. However, we insist that neither Christ's virgin birth nor His literal reign on earth can be spiritualized without doing violence to the laws of interpretation. This method of spiritualizing is enlarging the ranks of modernism, for when a theological student is taught that he is to spiritualize the Davidic throne in these passages, he may feel that he is justified in spiritualizing the virgin birth. The result has been that our protestant pulpits are occupied by men who are spiritualizing other important aspects of divine revelation

such as our Lord's Transfiguration, His miracles, His own bodily
Resurrection, hell, etc.

The Lamb and the Lion

The prophetic Scriptures present the Person and work of Christ
in full. He is seen coming meek as a sacrificial Lamb and mighty as
a resistless Lion. As the Lamb, the world was to see His sufferings;
as the Lion, it will be to view His sovereignty. After His Resurrection our Lord Himself said to the disciples on the Emmaus road,

> . . . O fools, and slow of heart to believe all that the prophets have
> spoken: Ought not Christ to have suffered these things, and to
> enter into his glory? (Luke 24:25, 26).

The Apostle Peter wrote concerning "the sufferings of Christ, and
the glory that should follow" (I Peter 1:11). These two events
blend perfectly with the two advents of Christ. Concerning His
first advent in meekness and humility, Zechariah prophesied,

> Rejoice greatly, O daughter of Zion; shout, O daughter of Jerusa-
> lem: behold, thy King cometh unto thee: he is just, and having
> salvation; lowly, and riding upon an ass, and upon a colt the foal
> of an ass (Zechariah 9:9).

In meekness, as the Lamb, He was to be led to the slaughter,

> He was oppressed, and he was afflicted, yet he opened not his
> mouth: he is brought as a lamb to the slaughter, and as a sheep
> before her shearers is dumb, so he openeth not his mouth (Isaiah
> 53:7).

The New Testament confirms the message of Isaiah as having direct
reference to Christ (Acts 8:32-35). The suffering, sacrificial Lamb
is the only Christ the world has known, therefore, it is imperative
that He come again to rule as King, the resistless, conquering "Lion
of the tribe of Juda, the Root of David, (who) hath prevailed"
(Revelation 5:5). The nations have not yet seen the fierceness of
His wrath, but "he shall rule them with a rod of iron." He is the
"KING OF KINGS, AND LORD OF LORDS" (Revelation 19:15,
16).

It was given to David to see this twofold revelation of Messiah.
Certain of the Messianic Psalms depict both scenes. Psalm 22 has
been called "The Psalm of the Saviour's Cross," while Psalm 24 is
"The Psalm of the Sovereign's Crown." In the former we see the
dying Lamb, while the latter sets forth the dominating Lion. Again
we read,

Reproach hath broken my heart; and I am full of heaviness: and I looked for some to take pity, but there was none; and for comforters, but I found none. They gave me also gall for my meat; and in my thirst they gave me vinegar to drink (Psalm 69:20, 21).

These prophecies, recorded by David, were literally fulfilled in the sufferings of Christ. But David, by the Holy Spirit, uttered another prophecy that awaits fulfillment when Christ comes back to earth with His saints,

My covenant will I not break, nor alter the thing that is gone out of my lips. Once have I sworn by my holiness that I will not lie unto David. His seed shall endure for ever, and his throne as the sun before me (Psalm 89:34-36).

The Davidic Covenant

In the field of eschatology, lecturers and writers sometimes fail to point out the importance of God's promise to David regarding David's posterity and his throne. Those who deny the inspiration of the Holy Scriptures ignore the subject entirely. But among our conservative brethren, who put forth honest effort in their interpretation of the Scriptures, there are those who either spiritualize the truth, or else satisfy themselves with the solution that the promises to David already have been fulfilled in Christ.

We pursue the subject in this chapter because we believe that the Davidic Covenant holds an important place in determining the purposes of God.

Let us read the covenant Jehovah made with David,

And when thy days be fulfilled, and thou shalt sleep with thy fathers, I will set up thy seed after thee, which shall proceed out of thy bowels, and I will establish his kingdom. He shall build an house for my name, and I will establish the throne of his kingdom for ever. I will be his father, and he shall be my son. If he commit iniquity, I will chasten him with the rod of men, and with the stripes of the children of men: But my mercy shall not depart away from him, as I took it from Saul, whom I put away before thee. And thine house and thy kingdom shall be established for ever before thee: thy throne shall be established for ever (II Samuel 7:12-16).

God had revealed to Nathan, the prophet, that He intended to build, through David's posterity, a throne and a kingdom that would not be overthrown. That such a kingdom has not been established, we are agreed. We do not see in this covenant the slightest obligation upon David. If David's posterity needed chastening, God would surely chasten them, but it is clear that the covenant could not be nullified. In the Psalms David praised God for this unconditional promise, for God had said,

> If his children forsake my law, and walk not in my judgments; If they break my statutes, and keep not my commandments; Then will I visit their transgression with the rod, and their iniquity with stripes. Nevertheless my loving-kindness will I not utterly take from him, nor suffer my faithfulness to fail. My covenant will I not break, nor alter the thing that is gone out of my lips. Once have I sworn by my holiness that I will not lie unto David. His seed shall endure for ever, and his throne as the sun before me (Psalm 89:30-36).

The Davidic covenant included the provision of a Son, yet to be born, who would establish David's kingdom and occupy his throne. Much that is written in the Bible found application and fulfillment in David's son, Solomon. But there were promises that were not for Solomon, nor for any other of David's sons of that generation. Upon David's death, Solomon ascended the throne. During his reign the Temple was erected, and he reigned in peace. But it all was only temporary. Solomon sinned, and his kingdom went into decline and was scattered. Surely that was not the everlasting kingdom that God had promised to David. But a greater than Solomon was yet to come. He, too, was David's Son, ". . . Jesus Christ, the Son of David . . ." (Matthew 1:1).

In the first sixteen verses of Matthew 1, there is traced for us a genealogy that shows how God has kept His word in raising up David's Son, and that Son is Jesus Christ who is shown to be the King legally. Mary, the mother of Jesus, was likewise a descendant of David, so that no matter how we view the birth of Christ, He is entitled to the throne of David. No doubt David had looked to Solomon for the fulfillment of God's plan to establish the kingdom, but Solomon ended in failure, so that David was disappointed in him.

Then David's Son, the greater than Solomon, was born. But where is the kingdom? One day He rode into the city of David to offer Himself to the people as their King. The crowds shouted,

> Blessed be the kingdom of our father David, that cometh in the name of the Lord: Hosanna in the highest (Mark 11:10).

But their cries were all hollow and unreal. Soon that same mob cried, "Crucify him," and His coming ended in crucifixion. But the grave could not hold Him. He arose triumphant and is seated at the right hand of the majesty on high, waiting. Waiting for what? Let David tell us.

> The LORD said unto my Lord, Sit thou at my right hand, until I make thine enemies thy footstool (Psalm 110:1).

The right to rule will never be transferred to any other. God has reserved that holy privilege for David's Son according to the flesh, our Lord Jesus Christ.

> (Which he had promised afore by his prophets in the holy scriptures,) Concerning his Son Jesus Christ our Lord, which was made of the seed of David according to the flesh (Romans 1:2, 3).

David's kingship and reign will one day find its full realization in our Lord Jesus Christ. After David had been anointed king, he suffered as the crownless king, dethroned. His enemies seemed to triumph for a while. But at last the time came when he triumphed over his enemies and they all were subdued before him. He broke their power and dealt with them in judgment, reigning in righteousness for a season.

> And David reigned over all Israel; and David executed judgment and justice unto all his people (II Samuel 8:15).

This is a type of our Lord Jesus Christ. His suffering, and the temporary conquest of His enemies over Israel, we have seen. But He will come again as the conquering, righteous King over all Israel. He will occupy the throne of David and shall judge the nations. God has decreed,

> . . . rule thou in the midst of thine enemies (Psalm 110:2).

It is God who will give to Jesus the throne of David from which ". . . he shall reign over the house of Jacob . . ." (Luke 1:33). This is that to which Jeremiah refers in his prophecy,

> Behold, the days come, saith the LORD, that I will raise unto David a righteous Branch, and a King shall reign and prosper, and shall execute judgment and justice in the earth. In his days Judah shall be saved, and Israel shall dwell safely: and this is his name whereby he shall be called, THE LORD OUR RIGHTEOUSNESS (Jeremiah 23:5, 6).

All will admit that the righteous Branch of David refers to Jesus Christ, and surely we must agree that the kingdom was not set up when Jesus was here on earth. When the Davidic covenant is fulfilled, men will not decide whether or not they will accept the kingdom and live by it. Man will have nothing to say about it. Christ shall rule with a rod of iron, and at the mention of His name, God has decreed that,

> . . . every knee should bow, of things in heaven, and things in earth, and things under the earth; And that every tongue should confess that Jesus Christ is Lord, to the glory of God the Father (Philippians 2:10, 11).

Most conservative theologians are agreed that the line which began with David has its final fulfillment and consummation in Jesus Christ. But the problem of the fulfillment has to do with *method* and *time*. John F. Walvoord has expressed it thus, "The problem of fulfillment does not consist in the question of whether Christ is the one who fulfills the promises, but rather on the issue of *how* Christ fulfills the covenant and *when* He fulfills it." The answers to this twofold question are closely related. One correlates to the other. If it is to be a literal kingdom on earth, then it is still future. If it is a spiritual kingdom, it might be past, present or future. However, if the fulfillment of the Davidic covenant is to be interpreted as spiritual and not literal, there are obvious difficulties which arise in the definition of the kingdom itself.

The writer sees in the Scriptures that Jesus Christ will come back to set up a kingdom on earth in which He, the King will reign in righteousness. When He comes, it will be the coming of the smiting Stone of Daniel's prophecy (Daniel 2:34, 35). The Stone did not fall from heaven when Jesus was born, as some would tell us. Nor can we locate the falling of the Stone in any succeeding century since Christ's birth. There must first be an empire of ten kings,

> And in the days of these kings shall the God of heaven set up a kingdom, which shall never be destroyed: and the kingdom shall not be left to other people, but it shall break in pieces and consume all these kingdoms, and it shall stand for ever (Daniel 2:44).

If the confederation of the ten-nation empire is in the making, and there are indications that it is, we may keep the upward look, for our redemption draweth nigh.

Before we look at some Scripture passages that distinguish the various thrones of our Lord, there is another significant statement in the Acts. I am thinking of three verses in chapter two.

> Men and brethren, let me freely speak unto you of the patriarch David, that he is both dead and buried, and his sepulchre is with

us unto this day. Therefore being a prophet, and knowing that God hath sworn with an oath to him, that of the fruit of his loins, according to the flesh, he would raise up Christ to sit on his throne; He seeing this before spake of the resurrection of Christ, that his soul was not left in hell, neither his flesh did see corruption (Acts 2:29-31).

The context, as we see it, does not permit a spiritualizing of this great sermon that Peter preached. Peter states clearly that God would raise up Jesus to sit on David's throne, and that all of this would be "according to the flesh" and not according to the spirit. When the Acts was written, our Lord Jesus was seated at the right hand of the Father. It is clear that He will remain there "until" He comes again to make His enemies His footstool (Acts 2:34, 35). When Jehovah had sworn with an oath to David that David's Son would reign upon his throne, it was certain to come to pass. God cannot deny Himself.

Thus saith the Lord; If ye can break my covenant of the day, and my covenant of the night, and that there should not be day and night in their season; Then may also my covenant be broken with David my servant, that he should not have a son to reign upon his throne . . . (Jeremiah 33:20, 21).

The Son of David was born, and unbelieving men nailed Him to the cross at Calvary. However, the divine arrangement of night and day had not been broken, so God raised Him from death and the grave that His oath should not fail. By faith David foresaw the Lord Jesus Christ always before his face, and in his faith he believed in Christ's Resurrection and subsequent kingship. Not only did David foresee the Resurrection of Christ, but by the Holy Spirit he also foretold it when he wrote,

For thou wilt not leave my soul in hell; neither wilt thou suffer thine Holy One to see corruption (Psalm 16:10).

Therefore being a prophet, and knowing that God had sworn with an oath to him, that of the fruit of his loins, according to the flesh, he would raise up Christ to sit on his throne; He seeing this before spake of the resurrection of Christ, that his soul was not left in hell, neither his flesh did see corruption (Acts 2:30, 31).

The Thrones of Our Lord

Several times in Scripture we read about the thrones of the Lord. Since God is eternal and had no beginning, we conclude that somewhere in heaven He has His eternal throne. David writes,

> The Lord is in his holy temple, the Lord's throne is in heaven. . . .
> (Psalm 11:4).

This is the throne that stood from all eternity in heaven, the eternal dwelling place of God. Doubtless the Son shared the eternal throne with the Father. When man by his disobedience became a guilty, lost sinner, the Son left the throne and came to this earth, His footstool. He exchanged His crown for the cross to purchase a lost world. Rising from the dead, He ascended on high where He is today, at the right hand of God, sharing His Father's throne.

But one day He will leave His Father's throne to return to earth for His bride. Then He will take His place upon the judgment seat, the *Bema* (tribunal), sometimes translated *throne* (Acts 12:21).

> . . . for we shall all stand before the judgment seat of Christ
> (Romans 14:10).

This has been called by some, "the award throne." Christ Himself will occupy it and will be the judge of the believer's works.

After He has finished judging the believer for his works, Christ will return to earth in visible glory and regal splendor, with His saints, where He will reign upon the throne of His glory.

> When the Son of man shall come in his glory, and all the holy angels with him, then shall he sit upon the throne of his glory: And before him shall be gathered all nations; and he shall separate them one from another, as a shepherd divideth his sheep from the goats: And he shall set the sheep on his right hand, but the goats on the left. Then shall the King say unto them on his right hand, Come, ye blessed of my Father, inherit the kingdom prepared for you from the foundation of the world (Matthew 25:31-34).

The nations mentioned here are the living nations (Gentiles), which are on the earth when our Lord returns with His own. This judgment of nations comes at the end of the time of Jacob's trouble, before the thousand years of kingdom blessing. The nations are judged for their treatment of the Jews, "my brethren" according to the flesh. Nowhere in the Scripture are we taught that this is a universal blessing.

Following the judgment of the nations, our Lord ascends the throne of David where He reigns over Israel. There are no Gentile blessings in view here. Paul said,

> Now I say that Jesus Christ was a minister of the circumcision for

the truth of God, to confirm the promises made unto the fathers (Romans 15:8).

The promises to Israel concerned her return to her own land, and Immanuel's reign over her promised kingdom. The disciples must have had this in mind when they asked,

> . . . Lord, wilt thou at this time restore again the kingdom to Israel? (Acts 1:6).

It was testified of Jesus that He was born "King of the Jews" (Matthew 2:2), and for making this claim He was put to death (Matthew 27:11, 27-29). All the prophecies concerning His life, death, and Resurrection have been fulfilled, and so Israel must yet see the return and reign of Messiah, her King. Like every other phase of Messiah's work, it was prophesied of old, and must therefore come to pass.

This reign will last for one thousand years, and Jerusalem will be the glorified capital of Christ's earthy kingdom as He sits upon the throne of His father David. Let us not lose sight of the fact that, from the time of Abraham, the sovereign purposes of God on earth were carried out through Israel nationally. Now we know that God's dealings with the world through Israel were interrupted when He permitted His chosen people to be taken captive into Babylon under Nebuchadnezzar in 606 B.C. This was the beginning of the Gentile world-rule which is to continue "until the fulness of the Gentiles be come in" (Romans 11:25). This ending of Gentile world-power will be marked by the coming again of Messiah, the Lord Jesus Christ. This is all arranged in order in Daniel's prophecy where we see,

> . . . that the stone was cut out of the mountain without hands, and that it brake in pieces the iron, the brass, the clay, the silver, and the gold . . . (Daniel 2:45).

Then the Gentiles from all the nations of the earth, who have persecuted God's chosen people, will be punished with everlasting punishment. God has not ceased to love His people Israel. To respect and care for the Jew is to honor God, for Jesus said,

> And the King shall answer and say unto them, Verily, I say unto you, Inasmuch as ye have done it unto one of the least of these my brethren, ye have done it unto me (Matthew 25:40).

When the King comes back He will provide an era of peace and righteousness for His people.

We hasten to mention two more thrones of Scripture in order that our readers may not be confused between these and David's throne. At the end of the Millennium, when all things have been subjected under His feet, Christ will occupy the Great White Throne (Revelation 20:11-15). This is the final judgment of the wicked dead who did not obey the Gospel of the Lord Jesus Christ and receive Him as Saviour. This is the dark hour for all who would not believe. What a tragic scene when all Christ-rejectors are cast into the lake of fire!

Then we have one final throne mentioned in the last chapter of the Bible. Here is a picture of the eternal state of the redeemed. There the throne of God is established in unquestioned authority,

> And there shall be no more curse: but the throne of God and of the Lamb shall be in it; and his servants shall serve him (Revelation 22:3).

This is His eternal throne from which He shall reign throughout eternity.

The People and the Land

The Millennial reign of Christ on the earth cannot be viewed aright unless we have a clear understanding of God's promises concerning Israel's land. Does Israel have an earthly possession? Indeed, yes! When God guided Abraham into Canaan He made this promise,

> . . . Unto thy seed will I give this land . . . (Genesis 12:7).

This was no mere casual mentioning of the earthly inheritance, for the promise was repeated several times. Later God had said,

> And I will give unto thee, and to thy seed after thee, the land wherein thou art a stranger, all the land of Canaan, for an everlasting possession; and I will be their God (Genesis 17:8).

This covenant was confirmed later to Isaac. Just before his death, Jacob told his son Joseph,

> . . . God Almighty appeared unto me at Luz in the land of Canaan, and blessed me, And said unto me, Behold, I will make thee fruitful, and multiply thee, and I will make of thee a multitude of people; and will give this land to thy seed after thee for an everlasting possession (Genesis 48:3, 4).

As we trace the history of Israel, we find episodes when the nation was separated from the Promised Land. I am thinking of those periods when the people were held in bondage by Pharaoh in Egypt, the dispersion of the ten tribes, the seventy-years captivity, and the present world-wide scattering of the Jew among all nations. But the Bible teaches, as we understand it, that there is hope for the seed of Abraham and the possession of the land. No one questions that God has punished His people for their unfaithfulness and disobedience, but the chastening of Jehovah does not disannul His promises that He, in mercy, will regather Israel to the Promised Land. Jeremiah prophesied,

> Behold, I will bring them from the north country, and gather them from the coasts of the earth. . . . He that scattered Israel will gather him, and keep him, as a shepherd doth his flock (Jeremiah 31:8, 10).

The Palestinian Covenant includes Israel's national conversion and restoration to the land, her national prosperity, and the suppression of all Israel's oppressors. The Holy Land is Israel's land, God's gift to that nation. When Israel is finally regathered from the nations of the world to the Promised Land, then Israel's King, "Immanuel," the Lord Jesus Christ, shall rule His people, for that Land is truly as Isaiah said,

> . . . Thy land, O Immanuel (Isaiah 8:8).

The City of Zion

An interesting word appearing well over 100 times in the Old Testament is *Zion*. In the Books of Psalms and Isaiah it is found most frequently. In the New Testament, the same term is used, only it is rendered as *Sion*. But how are we to interpret these references to Zion? In the mind of this writer there is no question about the reference meaning the earthly city of Jerusalem. Granted we read about the New Jerusalem in the Book of the Revelation, but under the Old Dispensation there was no thought of a heavenly Jerusalem. When Moses and the prophets spoke of Zion they were speaking in terms of an earthly, visible city. Anton Darms says, "This city was established by David upon Mount Zion as the abode of Jehovah, and was the theocratic center of divine government throughout all the earth. Even when used in a symbolic sense, Zion — meaning the Kingdom of God — always centers in the literal Jerusalem. Since Jerusalem is always the earthly Jerusalem unless otherwise clearly mentioned, so Mount Zion can be only earthly unless otherwise declared." Let us look at some of the references to Zion.

"Nevertheless David took the strong hold of Zion: the same is the city of David" (II Samuel 5:7). After King Saul's death, David was made king over all Israel. The Jebusites had taken Zion (Jerusalem), and had overthrown the worship of the true God, but David was determined to capture the fortress, and even though the Jebusites defied him, David took the stronghold of Zion and dedicated the city to the worship of Jehovah. So Zion was made the city of David, for,

> . . . David dwelt in the fort, and called it the city of David . . . (II Samuel 5:9).

David not only made Jerusalem the center of his rule, but it also became the central place of worship for the twelve tribes of Israel. That God should choose a place where sacrifice and offering would be made was not new to the Jew. He looked for such a place, for God had told Moses of His intention, and Moses in turn declared it to the people (Deuteronomy 12:5-7). This is "the city of David, which is Zion" (I Kings 8:1). There the worshiping Israelites rejoiced in Jehovah.

> Beautiful for situation, the joy of the whole earth, is mount Zion. . . (Psalm 48:2).

Now we know that the standards of worship, begun by David in Mount Zion, were not continued. Disobedience and decline in the nation brought on the Assyrian and Babylonian captivities, so that reproach instead of glory was brought upon Jehovah. But during the apostasy and captivity, God was speaking to His prophets concerning Zion's future. Isaiah prophesied,

> And the ransomed of the LORD shall return, and come to Zion with songs and everlasting joy upon their heads: they shall obtain joy and gladness, and sorrow and sighing shall flee away (Isaiah 35:10).
>
> Awake, awake; put on thy strength, O Zion; put on thy beautiful garments, O Jerusalem, the holy city: for henceforth there shall no more come into thee the uncircumcised and the unclean. Shake thyself from the dust; arise, and sit down, O Jerusalem: loose thyself from the bands of thy neck, O captive daughter of Zion. . . . How beautiful upon the mountains are the feet of him that bringeth good tidings, that publisheth peace; that bringeth good tidings of good, that publisheth salvation; that saith unto Zion, Thy God

reigneth! Thy watchmen shall lift up the voice; with the voice together shall they sing: for they shall see eye to eye, when the LORD shall bring again Zion. Break forth into joy, sing together, ye waste places of Jerusalem: for the LORD hath comforted his people, he hath redeemed Jerusalem. The LORD hath made bare his holy arm in the eyes of all the nations; and all the ends of the earth shall see the salvation of our God (Isaiah 52:1, 2, 7-10).

Here the prophet is declaring that Zion shall be redeemed, and the King shall come again to that city. When Jesus wept over Jerusalem, He was sad because of the rejection of His people, but we cannot help but feel that He was thinking somewhat of the city itself. Yet He assured His own that the desolation of Jerusalem was only for a time,

And they shall fall by the edge of the sword, and shall be led away captive into all nations: and Jerusalem shall be trodden down of the Gentiles, *until* the times of the Gentiles be fulfilled (Luke 21:24).

The Jews are scattered among the nations, and Palestine has been the storm-center of the Gentile nations but it is not for long, only

Until

. . . until the times of the Gentiles be fulfilled. Today Palestine is taking on new life. The day is not far away when Jesus will return as Israel's Messiah and King.

. . . Thus saith the LORD of hosts; I am jealous for Jerusalem and for Zion with a great jealousy. And I am very sore displeased, with the heathen that are at ease; for I was but a little displeased, and they helped forward the affliction. Therefore thus saith the LORD; I am returned to Jerusalem with mercies: my house shall be built in it, saith the LORD of hosts, and a line shall be stretched forth upon Jerusalem. Cry yet, saying, Thus saith the LORD of hosts; My cities through prosperity shall yet be spread abroad, and the LORD shall yet comfort Zion, and shall yet choose J e r u s a l e m (Zechariah 1:14-17).

Thus we have a picture of the coming kingdom of Christ, a kingdom in the earth, centered at Jerusalem. God is not through with the Jews. The King Himself, our Lord and Saviour Jesus Christ, was a Jew; the Scriptures were penned by the hands of Jewish writers; the mighty apostles were Jews. Christian, let us be the friend of the Jew. We should be the greatest friend that he has. God will restore the kingdom to Israel.

The Kingdom Described

(A) Satan Bound

The character of the Millennium is plainly described in God's Word. When our Lord returns to the earth with His own, Satan will be confined to the abyss for one thousand years,

> And I saw an angel come down from heaven, having the key of the bottomless pit and a great chain in his hand. And he laid hold on the dragon, that old serpent, which is the Devil, and Satan, and bound him a thousand years, And cast him into the bottomless pit, and shut him up, and set a seal upon him, that he should deceive the nations no more, till the thousand years should be fulfilled: and after that he must be loosed a little season (Revelation 20:1-3).

There can be no Golden Age on earth while the devil is free. Since he was cast out of heaven, Satan has been busy seeking to destroy everything that has in it the semblance of holiness and true righteousness. Since the fall of our first parents, man has never known what this world is like freed from the evil influences of the devil. All hatred and strife have been stirred up by the evil one, but during the Millennium, his power to operate shall be withheld.

Satan has been the world's greatest deceiver. From the creation of Adam and Eve, he has falsified the character of God and has misrepresented the plan of salvation, so that he is called "the Devil, and Satan, which deceiveth the whole world" (Revelation 12:9). During the thousand years, the whole earth is to be free from the presence and influence of its worst enemy. Those who think that the kingdom is to be ushered in through the preaching of the Gospel fail to see that a warless world in which righteousness and justice rule can never be a reality as long as Satan is free to carry out his wiles. The kingdom of the prince and the power of the air must be brought to nought before the kingdom of the Prince of peace can be brought to pass. The author of all evil, the father of lies, has duped some men into believing that evil in the earth will grow less and less until it has vanished completely. But this is not a doctrine of the Scriptures. Sin began with Satan, and it will run its course until Jesus Christ comes back again to restrain the wicked one.

The scene must be interpreted as literal. Some have argued against the literalness of this scene by asking how a chain of any metal can bind a spirit. In answer to this argument, Seiss says:

"The record does not say that it is a chain of iron, or brass, or steel, or any other material of earthly chains. It is a chain of divine making, as the sword that proceeds from the mouth of the Son of God. It is a chain of a character than can bind spirit and fetter angels. Jude tells of such chains, actually holding demons now (Jude 6), and which not even the angels can break." The chains by which Satan are bound are not the temporal chains of man's making, but the "everlasting chains" fashioned by God Himself.

The place into which Satan is cast for one thousand years is called "the bottomless pit," which is translated *the Abyss.* We are not to confuse the *Abyss* with hell. The general belief that Satan has been in hell is untrue. He has never been there, and he will not reach that lake of fire until after the Millennium (Revelation 20:10).

(B) Justice

Jeremiah prophesied,

> Behold, the days come, saith the LORD, that I will raise unto David a righteous Branch, and a King shall reign and prosper and shall execute judgment and justice in the earth (Jeremiah 23:5).

The world has seen little of true justice. That virtue which consists in giving to every one his due is seldom seen among men. The world could do with a demonstration of impartiality and equity. Even in our higher courts absolute justice is not always known. Many men have been fired with the ambition to rule the world. Lucifer was the first to aspire to world dominion, and it led to his downfall. No earthly potentate has conquered the world. Only our Lord Jesus Christ can claim this right.

Earthly rulers are biased and partial. But never is there injustice in heaven. The decisions of God are according to righteousness and justice. Human governments and courts may be sincere in their judgments, but they are not able to get the true facts in the case, so that they often are sincerely wrong. But in the Golden Age, the King is the omniscient One who knows all.

> With righteousness shall he judge the poor, and reprove with equity for the meek of the earth. . . (Isaiah 11:4).

No police forces nor witnesses will be needed by the King in the Golden Age. His own righteous laws will be in force, and violators will be dealt with justly and righteously. What glorious anticipation! Words fail us to express the delight and expectancy that is in our hearts!

(C) A Time of Safety

> But they shall sit every man under his vine and under his fig tree; and none shall make them afraid: for the mouth of the LORD of hosts hath spoken it (Micah 4:4).

> And I will make with them a covenant of peace, and will cause the evil beasts to cease out of the land, and they shall dwell safely in the wilderness, and sleep in the woods (Ezekiel 34:25).

> The wolf and the lamb shall feed together, and the lion shall eat straw like the bullock: and dust shall be the serpent's meat. They shall not hurt nor destroy in all my holy mountain, saith the LORD (Isaiah 65:25).

We have in these verses a remarkable description of the safety and security that will be enjoyed during the Kingdom Age. The King will see to it that we are exempt from hurt and injury. We will not need to fear bodily injury from the lower animal creation. The Creator of the animal kingdom will subdue His creatures so that no human need fear the wild beasts.

This safety will include our security from bodily sickness.

> And the inhabitant shall not say, I am sick: the people that dwell therein shall be forgiven their iniquity (Isaiah 33:24).

Of course, there will be some sickness in the Kingdom Age, but only for those who insist upon rebelling against God. Under ordinary circumstances, the gift of long life will be granted, so that those who willingly subject themselves to the King will enjoy long life such as the patriarchs enjoyed. While it will be possible for man to sin against God during the Millennium, his behavior will be excellent compared to what it is today with the adversary to tempt him. If a man dies at the age of an hundred, such a death will be looked upon as the death of a child,

> . . . for the child shall die an hundred years old. . . (Isaiah 65:20).

The world today is not a safe place in which to dwell. Thousands die every year from accidents, contagious diseases and murder. But the hand of the Lord will stay all this in the Millennium. The Kingdom Age will not be like the eternal state in which sin can never again strike in death, for God will act judicially in the Millennium against all who sin against Him. However, all who submit to His righteous rule will enjoy safety and security during that period. Before God has finished with this present world, He will permit man to dwell in safety, justice, and free from the temptation of the devil.

(D) A Warless World

Under the perfect rule of the Prince of Peace, we are assured that wars will cease and nations shall cease to teach the methods of warfare. Our present age has been like each preceding one, a time of bloodshed. Jesus said that wars and rumors of wars would characterize this present time. But in that day,

> . . . He shall judge among the nations, and shall rebuke many people: and they shall beat their swords into plowshares, and their spears into pruninghooks: nation shall not lift up sword against nation, neither shall they learn war any more (Isaiah 2:4).

Many times man has attempted to bring about world peace. Statesmen realize that the improved methods of communication and transportation, and the interdependence of nations, mean that those nations must enjoy more peaceful relations if they are to survive. But we know to date that every effort of man to bring about permanent world peace has ended in failure. Neither civilization, organized religion, nor human government have been able to silence the war drums. It is utter foolishness to talk about bringing in the Kingdom in a world where Satan is loose. Wherever there is a reign of perfect peace, it follows that God's will must be carried out. When Jesus came to earth the first time, it was to reveal the will of God to man, but man would not have it. However, when He comes again in glory, it will be to establish the will of God whether man wants it or not.

Men do not want the authority of God established in the earth, because they must then relinquish their own authority in its place. Therefore, there will be wars and rumors of wars until the King returns to establish the authority of Jehovah over all other authorities and kingdoms (see Daniel 2:35; Zechariah 8:3). As this age draws toward its close, these wars and rumors of wars will intensify in frequency and size. Peace treaties will contain statements about a war to end all wars, according to their planning. But permanent peace will not come until the Prince of Peace comes to take over the reins of government. The only hope for the world is the return of the Lord Jesus Christ.

(E) A Change in the Animal Creation

When the kingdom is established, even the lower creation will be affected by it. Isaiah says,

> The wolf also shall dwell with the lamb, and the leopard shall lie down with the kid; and the calf and the young lion and the fatling together; and a little child shall lead them. And the cow and the bear shall feed; their young ones shall lie down together: and the lion shall eat straw like the ox (Isaiah 11:6, 7).

> The wolf and the lamb shall feed together, and the lion shall eat straw like the bullock: and dust shall be the serpent's meat . . . (Isaiah 65:25).

Human prose and poetry have dreamed about such conditions, but only divine inspiration has been able to depict it. Among the animal creation today we know that the law of survival of the fittest is in operation, but in earth's Golden Age, that law will cease to operate.

There is no indication in Scripture that the first Adam had any fear of beasts before the fall. But with the coming of Satan, sin entered, and since the fall man has feared wild beasts, particularly the serpent. There is not the slightest suggestion, however, that our Lord Jesus Christ, the last Adam, ever feared wild beasts. He was in the wilderness forty days, "with the wild beasts" (Mark 1:13), and that without fear. He, the Creator, never feared His creatures. They always have been under His dominion. He was Master of the situation when He rode the unbroken colt into Jerusalem. Even so will it be when He comes again to reign.

(F) "All Shall Know Me"

In the epistle to the Hebrews, it should be noted that the New Covenant looks ahead to the Millennium when the whole house of Israel shall know Messiah. God had said through the mouth of His prophet,

> The ox knoweth his owner, and the ass his master's crib: but *Israel doth not know* . . . (Isaiah 1:3).

Happily for the Christian, we know Him, but in that day,

> . . . the earth shall be filled with the knowledge of the glory of the Lord, as the waters cover the sea (Habakkuk 2:14).

It is the time, saith the Lord, when

> . . . they shall not teach every man his neighbor, and every man his brother, saying, Know the Lord: for all shall know me, from the least to the greatest (Hebrews 8:11).

While the New Covenant has a spiritual significance, it extends to the millennial blessing on earth when all men shall know the Lord. Our age makes much of the philosophy, "Know thyself," but the sum of all blessings is to "Know God." Under the dispensation of law, man could know himself, and while the law was holy and just and good, and revealed the requirements of God, it did not reveal God Himself. So what the law could not do, our Lord Jesus Christ accomplished. He came to reveal God that men might know Him. His first coming was rejected, so that men are still ignorant of the Almighty. But when He comes in kingly glory, the great desire and determination of God to be known by His own will be completed. The knowledge of God is one of the great Messianic blessings of the Kingdom Age. From the youngest and most illiterate to the oldest and most intellectual, theirs shall be the possession of the secret of blessing, that is, the personal knowledge of God.

There will be no further need for evangelizing the world then, for the world will be under the control of the King of kings, the Author of the evangel. Wherever one travels, he will not be able to find a single trace of heathen darkness and superstition. All people shall have a full knowledge of God, and His salvation will be known to the uttermost part of the earth. It is the day when,

> . . . at the name of Jesus every knee should bow. . . And that every tongue should confess that Jesus Christ is Lord, to the glory of God the Father (Philippians 2:10, 11).

Chapter 6

The End of This Present World

In the third chapter of the second epistle of Peter the Holy Spirit records the fact of three worlds. The *first* is identified by the words, "the world that then was" (verse 6); the *second* is clearly marked out as "the heavens and the earth, which are now" (verse 7); the *third* is seen in the prediction, "Nevertheless we, according to his promise, look for new heavens and a new earth, wherein dwelleth righteousness" (verse 13). You will notice that these three worlds are related to the three tenses of time, so that we see the *past* world, the *present* world, and the *prospective* world.

The Past World

A. The past world was *created* by God. The first thing our chapter says about the old world is that "by the word of God the heavens were of old, and the earth standing out of the water and in the water" (verse 5). The heavens and the earth were created by the divine fiat, by God's authoritative decree. How did the world come into being? Certainly not by accident, nor by an evolutionary gathering of atoms. The eternal, omnipotent God commanded, and the world came into existence. The Psalmist said, "By the word of the LORD were the heavens made; and all the host of them by the breath of his mouth. . . . For he spake, and it was done; he commanded, and it stood fast" (Psalm 33:6, 9). Not less than nine times in Genesis 1 we read the words *"and God said"* in connection with the historical account of creation, and each time there follows the inevitable result, *"and it was so"* (verses 3, 6, 9, 11, 14, 20, 24, 26, 29). Indeed, "The voice of the LORD is powerful" (Psalm 29:4). Of course, no man was present to witness just how God did it, but "Through faith we understand that the worlds were framed by the word of God. . ." (Hebrews 11:3).

A closer look at II Peter 3 teaches us that we are not to be surprised at the rise of scoffers and sceptics (verses 3, 4). Their increase will characterize the last days, but their ignorance of the Biblical account of creation is a willful ignorance, "for this they willingly are ignorant of" (verse 5). There are many learned men who are educated beyond their own intellect and who totally ignore or else ridicule the teaching of the Bible on these as well as other matters. Some of these men are reputed to be scientists and expert in their respective fields. Such men, with their much learning, are dangerous, and the Bible warns the Christian to avoid such "vain babblings (i.e., empty voices), and oppositions of science falsely so called" (I Timothy 6:20). True science is never out of harmony with what the Bible teaches. When the truth of God's Word on this subject escapes the notice of a scientist so-called, it is because he wants it to do so. But it is the height of folly for men, with all their boasted knowledge, to attempt to bolster their willful unbelief by deliberately and knowingly sidestepping the plain statements of God's Word.

We know that the world was created, and is controlled (Hebrews 1:3) by the power of God's Word. If there were secondary causes, they derived their power from Him. The Bible opens with ten simple words which attribute the known world to God. They are, "In the beginning God created the heaven and the earth" (Genesis 1:1). While these words are remarkable for their simplicity, to many persons they have become sadly complicated by human speculations and theories. This first verse in Genesis speaks of the creation of all things, of world-stuff and physical matter, and the word "create" here is used in its highest sense. While all substance had a beginning, and thus is not eternal, in respect of time it is without date. I have no idea how old the original creation is. If we should learn that the work of creation stated in Genesis 1:1 dates back billions of years, I see no problem at all. When anyone asks me, "What or when was the beginning of things?" I respond with one pointed and pithy answer, "In the beginning God created the heaven and the earth." I am forever free from wearisome controversies and disputes regarding the origin of things and the authority of the Scriptures. The doctrine of creation by God according to the Bible is fundamental to historic Christianity, and this Scriptural record should settle the matter once and for all time. The world was created by God.

B. The past world was *condemned* by God. The Apostle Peter continues, "Whereby the world that then was, being overflowed with water, perished" (verse 6). This verse has reference to the Flood of Noah's day. The word "overflowed" is the translation of the Greek word *katakluzo,* meaning to inundate, deluge, submerge, overwhelm with water. From *katakluzo* we get our English word "cataclysm."

There is an abundance of evidence to support what the Bible teaches about the Flood in Noah's time. Here in our own United States geologists have discovered a strata of crushed seashells and fish fossils many miles from any body of water. Then, too, human skeletons have been found deep down in the earth, far below the depth where they would normally be buried. All of this is the result of a "cataclysm," a judgment by water. Dr. J. Vernon McGee makes the point that, as one looks out at the world of nature, he does not discover the love of God, only divine judgment. Nature has a bloody tooth and a very sharp claw. We witness it in earthquakes, tidal waves, floods, hurricanes and tornadoes. The only place where you will find the love of God is at Calvary where God was in Christ reconciling lost sinners to Himself.

Our Lord describes the condition of men's hearts and minds in that world of Noah's day — "For as in the days that were before the flood they were eating and drinking, marrying and giving in marriage, until the day that Noah entered into the ark. And knew not until the flood came, and took them all away; so shall also the coming of the Son of man be" (Matthew 24:38, 39). Now there is nothing sinful about eating, drinking and marrying. Food and water are necessary to man's existence, and marriage was instituted by God. Christ is saying in spite of Noah's faithful preaching for one hundred and twenty years, warning the people of imminent danger, they were apathetic and indifferent to the coming judgment, but instead pursued the normal things of life. Then the Flood came and God judged the human race.

Some critics have attacked the record of the Flood as false, using as a basis of argument the word "perish." They insist that if there were such a flood the earth still stands and therefore did not perish. But they are in error. The word "perish" (Gr. *apollumi*) does not mean extinction or annihilation, but loss, not of being, but of well-being. Jesus said that "whosoever believeth in him should not *perish*, but have everlasting life" (John 3:16). The person who dies in unbelief is said to perish, meaning that he loses his eternal well-being. Man was created by God to an eternal conscious existence. If he chooses heaven he is certain of eternal well-being; if he chooses hell he is certain of eternal torment having lost his well-being. Our Lord assured His followers who trust Him, "I give unto them eternal life; and they shall never *perish*" (John 10:28). In our chapter (II Peter 3) which discusses the three worlds, Peter says, "The Lord is . . . not willing that any should *perish*, but that all should come to repentance" (verse 9).

Just as surely as the earth was created by God, even so was it condemned by God by means of a watery judgment. The record stands and cannot be disproved. To deny it will never alter the facts. We have stressed these two historical facts, namely the creation and judgment of the earth by God, because we feel they are basic and essential as the foundation to the rest of our study. This is God's world, and any disposition He chooses to make of it must be a right choice on His part.

We shall now examine what the Apostle Peter has to say about

The Present World

A. The present world is a *contemptuous* world. "Knowing this first, that there shall come in the last days scoffers, walking after their own lusts, And saying, Where is the promise of his coming? for since the fathers fell asleep, all things continue as they were from the beginning of creation" (verses 3, 4). The present world system looks with scorn and ridicule upon these truths in God's Word. Their scoffing is aimed at the idea of the return of Jesus Christ to the earth and of coming judgment. Their minds are controlled by the ancient philosophy of *laissez faire,* the let-alone, non-interference principle. They rebel at the thought of God interfering with their selfish way of life. Men who walk "after their own lusts" resent anyone telling them that they are wrong. Thus they hold the Word of God in contempt because it pronounces judgment upon their evil way of life. They want nothing whatever to do with the disturbing idea of the return of Jesus Christ and the end of the world.

Such contempt for God and His Word is no new thing. It prevailed in Noah's day prior to the divine judgment of the Flood. "By faith Noah, being warned of God of things not seen as yet, moved with fear, prepared an ark to the saving of his house; by the which he condemned the world, and became heir of the righteousness which is by faith" (Hebrews 11:7). Every student should read from time to time the record of the Flood in Genesis 6-9. No doubt in Noah's time the scoffers were asking, "Where is the flood you have been predicting?" Peter said that men will be asking, "Where is the promise of His (Christ's) coming?" The question was a form of expression which implied that the thing being questioned did not so much as exist. In Malachi's day men were asking, "Where is the God of judgment?" (Malachi 2:17). When the Psalmist was in sorrow the heathen demanded of him, "Where is thy God?" (Psalm 42:3). The enemies of God said to His weeping prophet, "Where is the word of the LORD?" (Jeremiah 17:15).

The opponents of the prophecy in Peter's passage are demanding to know what has happened to the promise of Christ's coming. They regard the Second Coming of Christ in judgment as something that would have happened long ago if it was going to happen at all. They agreed that their ancestors lived and died and the world is going on precisely as it did in years past, without convulsive upheavals, so why should not this stable universe continue like this?

Actually they are suggesting that God made a promise and did not keep His word; He was tardy, or dilatory.

Peter's response is a moving one. First, he reminds all scoffers that man does not see time as God sees it. "One day is with the Lord as a thousand years, and a thousand years as one day" (verse 8). Here Peter applies the language of Psalm 90:4 which sets forth in striking contrast the difference between the divine and the human viewpoints of time. Neither Peter nor the Psalmist are saying that one day is as a thousand years, and a thousand years as one day, but that *"with the Lord"* one day is as a thousand years, and a thousand years as one day. Now when God speaks to man in terms of a thousand years (see Revelation 20:2-7), He means "a thousand years" because this is a term by which man reckons time. But with God, who is eternal, time does not exist.

Peter then goes on to tell the scoffers that any apparent slowness on God's part to send Jesus Christ to earth to judge was an act of mercy on His part. "The Lord is not slack concerning his promise, as some men count slackness; but is longsuffering to us-ward, not willing that any should perish, but that all should come to repentance" (verse 9). Any delay in the Second Coming of Jesus Christ is to give sinners a chance to repent and find salvation. Delay does not spring from any inability with God to carry out His promise, but instead that sinners should not perish.

Our world is not eternally stable and things are not forever the same. Any man who builds his hopes on the idea that this is a stable and unchanging universe is deluded and wrong. The old world perished in the flood, so do not hold this great historical truth in contempt.

B. The present world is a *condemned* world. As the past world was judged with water, so the present world will be judged with fire. "But the heavens and the earth, which are now, by the same word are kept in store, reserved unto fire against the day of judgment and perdition of ungodly men" (verse 7). This verse is stating a fact which has been sustained by accurate scientific discovery, namely, the present heaven and earth have in them a deposit of fire. This present condition of being stored up with fire is being constantly maintained and guarded. That the fire is there no true scientist will deny.

But who put it there, and how and why is it maintained? The answers are clearly unmistakable. "*By the word of God*" the heavens and the earth of old came into being, and "*by the same word*" the present heavens and earth are stored up with fire reserved for the day of judgment when Christ comes again (verses 5, 7). By His word were all things *created* (Psalm 33:6, 9); by His word are all things *controlled* (Hebrews 1:3 cf. Mark 4:39); by His word will the heavens and the earth be *condemned*. One single word from our blessed Lord, and this present order of things, which is but temporary, will meet a fiery doom.

The God of the Bible is the God of the atom. "Our God is a consuming fire" (Hebrews 12:29). There are many passages in the Bible which present Jehovah as the God of the fire:

The Presence of God in the Fire (Exodus 3:1-4).
The Pathway of God in the Fire (Exodus 13:21).
The Precepts of God in the Fire (Exodus 19:18; 20:1-17).
The Power of God in the Fire (I Kings 18:30-39).
The Protection of God in the Fire (Isaiah 43:2; Daniel 3:25).
The Punishment of God in the Fire (Genesis 19:23, 24; Leviticus 10:1, 2).

The Old Testament prophets foresaw a time when God would once again punish the earth with fire. The Psalmist presents a word picture of that day when he writes, "Our God shall come, and shall not keep silence: a fire shall devour before him, and it shall be very tempestuous round about him" (Psalm 50:3). Isaiah wrote, "Thou shalt be visited of the LORD of hosts with thunder, and with earthquake, and great noise, with storm and tempest, and the flame of devouring fire" (Isaiah 29:6). "And the LORD shall cause his glorious voice to be heard, and shall shew the lighting down of his arm, with the indignation of his anger, and with the flame of a devouring fire, with scattering, and tempest, and hailstones" (Isaiah 30:30). "For, behold, the LORD will come with fire, and with his chariots like a whirlwind, to render his anger with fury, and his rebuke with flames of fire. For by fire and by his sword will the LORD plead with all flesh: and the slain of the LORD shall be many" (Isaiah 66:15, 16). Joel adds, "And I will shew wonders in the heavens and in the earth, blood, and fire, and pillars of smoke" (Joel 2:30). Nahum said, "The mountains quake at him and the hills melt, and the earth is burned at his presence, yea, the world, and all that dwell therein. Who can stand before his indignation? and who can abide in the fierceness of his anger? his fury is poured out like fire, and the rocks are thrown down by him" (Nahum 1:5, 6). And Malachi closes the Old Testament with the words, "For, behold, the day cometh, that shall burn as an oven; and all the proud, yea, and all that do wickedly, shall be stubble: and the day that cometh shall burn them up, saith the LORD of hosts, that it shall leave them neither root nor branch" (Malachi 4:1). Peter is in good company when he writes his prophecy of a coming fiery judgment, for he and they were inspired alike by the Holy Spirit. Peter and the prophets saw this present world destroyed with the conflagration of God.

Now we must observe closely this same striking prophecy as given by the Lord Jesus Himself. He said, "Likewise also as it was in the days of Lot; they did eat, they drank, they bought, they sold, they planted, they builded; But the same day that Lot went out of Sodom it rained fire and brimstone from heaven, and destroyed them all. Even thus shall it be in the day when the Son of man is revealed" (Luke 17:28-30). Here our Lord supports the historicity of the fiery judgment upon Sodom in the days of Lot, and then He adds, "Even thus shall it be in the day when the Son of man is revealed." Moses gave to us a vivid and scientifically accurate description of the Sodom incident. He wrote by divine inspiration, "The sun was risen upon the earth when Lot entered into Zoar. Then the LORD rained upon Sodom and upon Gomorrah brimstone and fire from the LORD out of heaven" (Genesis 19:23, 24). When did the Lord rain upon Sodom and Gomorrah brimstone and fire out of heaven? Note with much care the answer, "The sun was risen upon the earth." Now we know that the sun is made up of atoms, a scientifically proven fact. So then, God simply shook a few atoms on those wicked cities and they were reduced to ashes. Let "science falsely so called" (I Timothy 6:20) grapple with that one. In this instance history is a forerunner of prophecy. Coming events cast their shadows before them. The ashes of Sodom cry out that judgment is coming.

God promised Noah that there will never be another earth-wide flood (Genesis 9:8-11). But we are assured by God that He will judge and purge the present world with fire. The next event in

God's prophetic program will be the Day of Christ, or the Rapture of the Church (I Thessalonians 4:13-18). This will be followed by the Tribulation, a period of seven years, identified as the Seventieth Week of Daniel's prophecy (Daniel 9:24-27). Following that will be the millennial reign of Christ on the earth (Revelation 20:1-7). At the conclusion of the Millennium, the Great White Throne Judgment will take place (Revelation 20:11-15). This is the judgment of wicked men which will bring to pass the fiery condemnation of this present world, "the earth also and the works that are therein shall be burned up" (II Peter 3:10), "when the Lord Jesus shall be revealed from heaven with his mighty angels, in flaming fire taking vengeance on them that know not God, and that obey not the gospel of our Lord Jesus Christ" (II Thessalonians 1:7, 8). Those who mock at God's truth do so to their own doom.

This brings us to the conclusion of our present study, namely,

The Prospective World

A. The prospective world is *promised* by God. The trusting child of God has the blessed prospect of a better world. The past world was judged by God with water; the present world is moving toward a judgment by fire. "Nevertheless we, according to his promise, look for new heavens and a new earth, wherein dwelleth righteousness" (verse 13). Although fire will one day cause the heavens and the earth to melt, there will arise from those ruins new heavens and a new earth where sin will be done away forever.

Before we examine further Peter's passage, let us look at some inspired words from the pen of the Apostle John. In Revelation we read, "And I saw a new heaven and a new earth: for the first heaven and the first earth were passed away" (Revelation 21:1). The language here must be interpreted in the light of other Scriptures, because neither Peter nor John are suggesting that the present heavens and earth are to be destroyed, that is, annihilated so as to utterly disappear and be no more. The Psalmist exclaimed, "Thy faithfulness is unto all generations: thou hast established the earth, and it abideth" (Psalm 119:90). God said to Isaiah, "For, behold, I create new heavens and a new earth: and the former shall not be remembered, nor come to mind" (Isaiah 65:17). The teaching seems to be that the great burning and melting of the earth and the atmospheric heavens of which Peter writes speaks of purification. From the "perished" earth in the Flood of Noah's day there came a purged earth. And so God in telling us through Peter that from the conflagration that will come upon the earth and the heavens surrounding the earth, there will emerge a purified heavens and earth, purged from all evil and sin.

I suspect that some of my readers might be wondering what our Lord meant by His words, "Heaven and earth shall pass away" (Matthew 24:35). He meant much the same as Paul meant when he said of the believing sinner, "Therefore if any man be in Christ, he is a new creature: old things are passed away; behold, all things are become new" (II Corinthians 5:17). Jesus and Paul only used the word "regeneration," and each used it but once. The word "regeneration" means *a new order*. Our Lord used it in reference to a physical new order in the earth (Matthew 19:28); Paul used it in connection with a spiritual new order in the life of the believing sinner when he is born again (Titus 3:5). In neither instance is there an obliteration, an annihilation, an extinction, a cessation of being, but rather a purging and purifying of the old sinful order and the bringing in of the new.

Peter says that the prospective world is "according to his (God's) promise" (II Peter 3:13). This promise had been given by God centuries before Peter was directed of the Holy Spirit to write his epistle. God had said to Isaiah, "For, behold, I create new heavens and a new earth: and the former shall not be remembered, nor come to mind" (Isaiah 65:17). "For as the new heavens and the new earth, which I will make, shall remain before me, saith the Lord, so shall your seed and your name remain" (Isaiah 66:22). Now we know that God is faithful (I Corinthians 1:9; II Thessalonians 3:3), and therefore He will keep His promise (Hebrews 10:23). "For all the promises of God in him are yea, and in him Amen . . ." (II Corinthians 1:20). In the Promiser each promise finds its affirmation and accomplishment. God never commits Himself to anything that He does not intend to carry out. He has said it and He will do it. There are no circumstances nor forces that can hinder Him. The certainty of the divine promises is bound up in the very character of God. "The Lord is not slack concerning his promise. . . . The day of the Lord will come. . . . We, according to his promise, look for new heavens and a new earth, wherein dwelleth righteousness."

B. The prospective world is *purified* by God. The Apostle describes the new world as the place "wherein dwelleth righteousness" (II Peter 3:13). Because of Satan and the sinful heart of man, this present world is described by the Apostle Paul as an "evil world" (Galatians 1:4). But in the prospective world all evil will be removed. "And there shall in no wise enter into it any thing that defileth, neither whatsoever worketh abomination, or maketh a lie: but they which are written in the Lamb's book of life" (Revelation 21:27). In our present world righteousness is subdued and evil reigns; in the future world righteousness will reign and evil will be done away. No one can argue the point that righteousness is not at home in our world today. But in the coming new earth Peter says that righteousness "dwelleth" (Gr. *katoikeo*), "to be permanently at home." At the risk of being labeled a gloomy pessimist, I must remind you that there is very little right in this world, in spite of what many people are saying to the contrary. And now I must press upon you the fact that I am a glowing optimist, looking for God's new world in which righteousness alone dwells, and which will abide throughout all the eternal ages.

The world to come is described further by the Apostle John. "And God shall wipe away all tears from their eyes; and there shall be no more death, neither sorrow, nor crying, neither shall there be any more pain: for the former things are passed away" (Revelation 21:4). This one verse is a sermon in itself.

"God shall wipe away all tears from their eyes." The tears recall the sorrows and heartaches of the pilgrim life. Occasionally, there are tears of joy, but such an experience is rare. When you see people crying you do not associate their tears with some joyful experience. You know they weep because a hurt has come to them. But here in John's Apocalyptic vision we have a tearless world where God Himself wipes away all tears from the eyes of His people.

"And there shall be no more death." The history of death is a record of sin. Death followed sin (Genesis 2:17; Romans 5:12). Death is sin's wages (Romans 6:23). We have the sentence of death in ourselves (II Corinthians 1:9). Death worketh in us (II

Corinthians 4:12). It is appointed unto man once to die (Hebrews 9:27). Death is man's enemy and the last enemy to be destroyed (I Corinthians 15:26). But our Lord Jesus Christ holds the key of death (Revelation 1:18), and when the new world is established He will have locked the door that shuts out death forever.

"Neither sorrow, nor crying, neither shall there be any more pain." Think of it! Grief, mourning, lamentation and all distress will be done away with in the new world. There will be no need for the medical doctor, the osteopathic doctor, the chiropractic doctor, the psychiatric doctor, and all the rest of them. The new world will be so wonderful that we will never again give thought to the present world in which we now live.

My friend, are you saved? Have you received Jesus Christ as your Lord and Saviour? If not, your future world will be one of eternal torment. "But the fearful, and unbelieving, and the abominable, and murderers, and whoremongers, and sorcerers, and idolaters, and all liars, shall have their part in the lake which burneth with fire and brimstone: which is the second death" (Revelation 21:8).

Come to Christ at once!

Bibliography

Allis, Oswald, *Prophecy and the Church* (Presbyterian & Reformed: Nutley, New Jersey, 1945)

Bauman, Louis S., *Russian Events in the Light of Bible Prophecy* (Dunham: Grand Rapids, n.d.)

Blackstone, W. E., *Jesus Is Coming* (Revell: Westwood, New Jersey, n.d.)

Chafer, Lewis Sperry, *The Kingdom in History and Prophecy* (Dunham: Grand Rapids, 1915)

Dabold, F. V., *The Mystery of Iniquity* (Dabold)

DeHaan, M. R., *The Second Coming of Jesus* (Zondervan: Grand Rapids, 1944)

Evans, Robert L., *The Jew in the Plan of God* (Loizeaux: Neptune, New Jersey, 1950)

Feinberg, Charles L., *Focus on Prophecy* (Revell: Westwood, New Jersey, n.d.)

Graham, James R., *The Divine Unfolding* (Zondervan: Grand Rapids, n.d.)

Hislop, Alexander, *The Two Babylons* (Loizeaux: Neptune, New Jersey, 1932)

Ironside, H. A., *Lectures on the Revelation* (Loizeaux: Neptune, New Jersey, 1953)

King, Guy H., *The Fellowship* (Chr. Lit. Crusade: Ft. Washington, Pa., 1954)

Lacey, Harry, *God and the Nations* (Loizeaux: Neptune, New Jersey, n.d.)

McClain, Alva J., *The Greatness of the Kingdom* (Zondervan: Grand Rapids, n.d.)

McGee, J. Vernon, *Reveling Through Revelation* (McGee)

Pache, René, *The Return of Jesus Christ* (Moody Press: Chicago, n.d.)

Pember, G. H., *The Great Prophecies* (Hodder and Stoughton: London, n.d.)

Pentecost, J. Dwight, *Things to Come* (Dunham: Grand Rapids, 1958)

Ryrie, Charles E., *The Basis of Premillennial Faith* (Loizeaux: Neptune, New Jersey, 1954)

Sauer, Erich, *The Triumph of the Crucified* (Eerdmans: Grand Rapids, 1951)

Smith, Wilbur M., *This Atomic Age and the Word of God* (Wilde: Natick, Mass., n.d.)

——————, *World Crisis in the Light of Prophetic Scriptures* (Moody Press: Chicago, n.d.)

Urquhart, John, *The Wonders of Prophecy* (Christian Publications: Harrisburg, Pa., n.d.)

Walvoord, John F., *The Millennial Kingdom* (Dunham: Grand Rapids, 1959)

——————, *The Return of the Lord* (Dunham: Grand Rapids, 1955)

Wuest, Kenneth, *In These Last Days* (Eerdmans: Grand Rapids, 1954)